OLD MOORE'S

HOROSCOPE AND ASTRAL DIARY

ARIES

OLD MOORE'S

HOROSCOPE AND ASTRAL DIARY

ARIES

foulsham
LONDON • NEW YORK • TORONTO • SYDNEY

… # foulsham
The Publishing House, Bennetts Close,
Cippenham, Slough, Berks SL1 5AP, England

Foulsham books can be found in all good bookshops or direct from
www.foulsham.com

ISBN 13: 978-0-572-03239-5
ISBN 10: 0-572-03239-0

Copyright © 2006 W. Foulsham & Co. Ltd.

A CIP record for this book is available from the British Library

All rights reserved

The Copyright Act prohibits (subject to certain very limited exceptions) the making of copies of any copyright work or of a substantial part of such a work, including the making of copies by photocopying or similar process. Written permission to make a copy or copies must therefore normally be obtained from the publisher in advance. It is advisable also to consult the publisher if in any doubt as to the legality of any copying which is to be undertaken.

Printed in Great Britain by Cox & Wyman Ltd, Reading, Berkshire.

CONTENTS

1	Introduction	6
2	The Essence of Aries: Exploring the Personality of Aries the Ram	7
3	Aries on the Cusp	12
4	Aries and its Ascendants	14
5	The Moon and the Part it Plays in your Life	21
6	Moon Signs	25
7	Aries in Love	29
8	Venus: The Planet of Love	32
9	Venus through the Zodiac Signs	34
10	The Astral Diary: How the Diagrams Work	38
11	Aries: Your Year in Brief	40
12	Aries 2007: Diary Pages	41
13	Rising Signs for Aries	158
14	The Zodiac, Planets and Correspondences	159

INTRODUCTION

Astrology has been a part of life for centuries now, and no matter how technological our lives become, it seems that it never diminishes in popularity. For thousands of years people have been gazing up at the star-clad heavens and seeing their own activities and proclivities reflected in the movement of those little points of light. Across centuries countless hours have been spent studying the way our natures, activities and decisions seem to be paralleled by their predictable movements. Old Moore, a time-served veteran in astrological research, continues to monitor the zodiac and has produced the Astral Diary for 2007, tailor-made to your own astrological make-up.

Old Moore's Astral Diary is unique in its ability to get to the heart of your nature and to offer you the sort of advice that might come from a trusted friend. The Diaries are structured in such a way that you can see in a day-by-day sense exactly how the planets are working for you. The diary section advises how you can get the best from upcoming situations and allows you to plan ahead successfully. There is room in the daily sections to put your own observations or even appointments, and the book is conveniently structured to stay with you throughout the year.

Whilst other popular astrology books merely deal with your astrological 'Sun sign', the Astral Diaries go much further. Every person on the planet is unique, and Old Moore allows you to access your individuality in a number of ways. The front section gives you the chance to work out the placement of the Moon at the time of your birth and to see how its position has set an important seal on your overall nature. Perhaps most important of all, you can use the Astral Diary to discover your Rising Sign. This is the zodiac sign that was appearing over the Eastern horizon at the time of your birth and is just as important to you as an individual as is your Sun sign.

It is the synthesis of many different astrological possibilities that makes you what you are, and with the Astral Diaries you can learn so much. How do you react to love and romance? Through the unique Venus tables and the readings that follow them, you can learn where the planet Venus was at the time of your birth. It is even possible to register when little Mercury appears to be running retrograde, which can explain why you sometimes feel chatty, whilst at other moments you would rather withdraw into yourself. The Astral Diary will be an interest and a support throughout the whole year ahead.

Old Moore extends his customary greeting to all people of the Earth and offers his age-old wishes for a happy and prosperous period ahead.

THE ESSENCE OF ARIES

Exploring the Personality of Aries the Ram

(21ST MARCH – 20TH APRIL)

What's in a sign?

Aries is not the first sign of the zodiac by accident. It's the place in the year when the spring begins, and so it represents some of the most dynamic forces in nature, and within the zodiac as a whole. As a result the very essence of your nature is geared towards promoting yourself in life and pushing your ideas forward very positively. You don't brook a great deal of interference in your life, but you are quite willing to help others as much as you can, provided that to do so doesn't curb your natural desire to get on in life.

Aries people are not universally liked, though your true friends remain loyal to you under almost any circumstances. But why should it be that such a dynamic and go-getting person does meet with some opposition? The answer is simple: not everyone is quite so sure of themselves as you are and many tend to get nervous when faced with the sheer power of the Aries personality. If there is one factor within your own control that could counter these problems it is the adoption of some humility – that commodity which is so important for you to dredge from the depths of your nature. If you only show the world that you are human, and that you are well aware of the fact, most people would follow you willingly to the very gates of hell. The most successful Aries subjects know this fact and cultivate it to the full.

Your executive skills are never in doubt and you can get almost anything practical done whilst others are still jumping from foot to foot. That's why you are such a good organiser and are so likely to be out there at the front of any venture. Adventurous and quite willing to show your bravery in public, you can even surprise yourself sometimes with the limits you are likely to go to in order to reach solutions that seem right to you.

Kind to those you take to, you can be universally loved when working at your best. Despite this there will be times in your life when you simply can't understand why some people just don't like you. Maybe there's an element of jealousy involved.

Aries resources

The part of the zodiac occupied by the sign of Aries has, for many centuries, been recognised as the home of self-awareness. This means that there isn't a person anywhere else in the zodiac that has a better knowledge of self than you do. But this isn't necessarily an intellectual process with Aries, more a response to the very blood that is coursing through your veins. Aries' success doesn't so much come from spending hours working out the pros and cons of any given course of action, more from the thrill of actually getting stuck in. If you find yourself forced into a life that means constantly having to think everything through to the tiniest detail, there is likely to be some frustration in evidence.

Aries is ruled by Mars, arguably the most go-getting of all the planets in the solar system. Mars is martial and demands practical ways of expressing latent power. It also requires absolute obedience from subordinates. When this is forthcoming, Aries individuals are the most magnanimous people to be found anywhere. Loyalty is not a problem and there have been many instances in history when Aries people were quite willing to die for their friends if necessary.

When other people are willing to give up and go with the flow, you will still be out there pitching for the result that seems most advantageous to you. It isn't something you can particularly control and those who don't know you well could find you sometimes curt and over-demanding as a result. But because you are tenacious you can pick the bones out of any situation and will usually arrive at your desired destination, if you don't collapse with fatigue on the way.

Routines, or having to take life at the pace of less motivated types, won't suit you at all. Imprisonment of any sort, even in a failed relationship, is sheer torture and you will move heaven and earth to get out into the big, wide world, where you can exploit your natural potential to the full. Few people know you really well because you don't always explain yourself adequately. The ones who do adore you.

Beneath the surface

Whereas some zodiac signs are likely to spend a great deal of their lives looking carefully at the innermost recesses of their own minds, Aries individuals tend to prefer the cut and thrust of the practical world. Aries people are not natural philosophers, but that doesn't mean that you aren't just as complicated beneath the surface as any of your astrological brothers and sisters. So what is it that makes the Aries firebrand think and act in the way that it does? To a great extent it is a lack of basic self-confidence.

This statement might seem rather odd, bearing in mind that a fair percentage of the people running our world were born under the sign of the Ram, but it is true nevertheless. Why? Because people who know themselves and their capabilities really well don't feel the constant need to prove themselves in the way that is the driving force of your zodiac sign. Not that your naturally progressive tendencies are a fault. On the contrary, if used correctly they can help you to create a much better, fairer and happier world, at least in your own vicinity.

The fact that you occasionally take your ball and go home if you can't get your own way is really down to the same insecurity that is noticeable through many facets of your nature. If Aries can't rule, it often doesn't want to play at all. A deep resentment and a brooding quality can build up in the minds and souls of some thwarted Aries types, a tendency that you need to combat. Better by far to try and compromise, itself a word that doesn't exist in the vocabularies of the least enlightened people born under the sign of the Ram. Once this lesson is learned, inner happiness increases and you relax into your life much more.

The way you think about others is directly related to the way you consider they think about you. This leads to another surprising fact regarding the zodiac sign. Aries people absolutely hate to be disliked, though they would move heaven and earth to prove that this isn't the case. And as a result Aries both loves and hates with a passion. Deep inside you can sometimes be a child shivering in the dark. If you only realise this fact your path to happiness and success is almost assured. Of course to do so takes a good deal of courage – but that's a commodity you don't lack.

Making the best of yourself

It would be quite clear to any observer that you are not the sort of person who likes to hang around at the back of a queue, or who would relish constantly taking orders from people who may not know situations as well as you do. For that reason alone you are better in positions that see you out there at the front, giving commands and enjoying the cut and thrust of everyday life. In a career sense this means that whatever you do you are happiest telling those around you how to do it too. Many Aries people quite naturally find their way to the top of the tree and don't usually have too much trouble staying there.

It is important to remember, however, that there is another side to your nature: the giving qualities beneath your natural dominance. You can always be around when people need you the most, encouraging and even gently pushing when it is necessary. By keeping friends and being willing to nurture relationships across a broad spectrum, you gradually get to know what makes those around you tick. This makes for a more patient and understanding sort of Aries subject – the most potent of all.

Even your resilience is not endless, which is why it is important to remember that there are times when you need rest. Bearing in mind that you are not superhuman is the hardest lesson to learn, but the admission brings humility, something that Aries needs to cultivate whenever possible.

Try to avoid living a restricted life and make your social contacts frequent and important. Realise that there is much more to life than work and spend some of your free time genuinely attempting to help those who are less well off than you are. Crucially you must remember that 'help' is not the same as domination.

The impressions you give

This section may well be of less interest to Aries subjects than it would be to certain other zodiac signs. The reason is quite clear. Aries people are far less interested in what others think about them than almost anyone else – or at least they tell themselves that they are. Either way it is counterproductive to ignore the opinions of the world at large because to do so creates stumbling blocks, even in a practical sense.

Those around you probably find you extremely capable and well able to deal with almost any situation that comes your way. Most are willing to rely heavily on you and the majority would almost instinctively see you as a leader. Whether or not they like you at the same time is really dependent on the way you handle situations. That's the difference between the go-getting, sometimes selfish type of Aries subject and the more enlightened amongst this illustrious sign.

You are viewed as being exciting and well able to raise enthusiasm for almost any project that takes your fancy. Of course this implies a great responsibility because you are always expected to come up with the goods. The world tends to put certain people on a pedestal, and you are one of them. On the other side of the coin we are all inclined to fire arrows at the elevated, so maintaining your position isn't very easy.

Most of the time you are seen as being magnanimous and kind, factors that you can exploit, whilst at the same time recognising the depth of the responsibility that comes with being an Aries subject. It might not be a bad thing to allow those around you to see that you too have feet of clay. This will make them respect and support you all the more, and even Aries people really do need to feel loved. A well-balanced Aries subject is one of the most elevated spirits to be found anywhere.

The way forward

You certainly enjoy life more when looking at it from the top of the tree. Struggling to get by is not in the least interesting to your zodiac sign and you can soon become miserable if things are not going well for you. That's why it is probably quite justified in your case to work tenaciously in order to achieve your objectives. Ideally, once you have realised some sort of success and security for yourself, you should then be willing to sit and watch life go by a little more. In fact this doesn't happen. The reason for this is clear. The Aries subject who learns how to succeed rarely knows when to stop – it's as simple as that.

Splitting your life into different components can help, if only because this means that you don't get the various elements mixed up. So, for example, don't confuse your love life with your professional needs, or your family with colleagues. This process allows you to view life in manageable chunks and also makes it possible for you to realise when any one of them may be working well. As a result you will put the effort where it's needed, and enjoy what is going well for you.

If you want to know real happiness you will also have to learn that acquisition for its own sake brings hollow rewards at best. When your talents are being turned outward to the world at large, you are one of the most potent and successful people around. What is more you should find yourself to be a much happier person when you are lending a hand to the wider world. This is possible, maybe outside of your normal professional sphere, though even where voluntary work is concerned it is important not to push yourself to the point of fatigue.

Keep yourself physically fit, without necessarily expecting that you can run to the South Pole and back, and stay away from too many stimulants, such as alcohol and nicotine. The fact is that you are best when living a healthy life, but it doesn't help either if you make even abstinence into an art form. Balance is important, as is moderation – itself a word that is difficult for you to understand. In terms of your approach to other people it's important to realise that everyone has a specific point of view. These might be different to yours, but they are not necessarily wrong. Sort out the friends who are most important to you and stick with them, whilst at the same time realising that almost everyone can be a pal – with just a little effort.

ARIES ON THE CUSP

Old Moore is often asked how astrological profiles are altered for those people born at either the beginning or the end of a zodiac sign, or, more properly, on the cusps of a sign. In the case of Aries this would be on the 21st of March and for two or three days after, and similarly at the end of the sign, probably from the 18th to the 20th of April. In this year's Astral Diaries, once again, Old Moore sets out to explain the differences regarding cuspid signs.

The Pisces Cusp – March 21st to March 24th

With the Sun so close to the zodiac sign of Pisces at the time you were born, it is distinctly possible that you have always had some doubts when reading a character breakdown written specifically for the sign of Aries. This isn't surprising because no zodiac sign has a definite start or end, they merely merge together. As a result there are some of the characteristics of the sign of the Fishes that are intermingled with the qualities of Aries in your nature.

What we probably find, as a result, is a greater degree of emotional sensitivity and a tendency to be more cognisant of what the rest of humanity is feeling. This is not to imply that Aries is unfeeling, but rather that Pisceans actively make humanity their business.

You are still able to achieve your most desired objectives in the practical world, but on the way, you stop to listen to the heartbeat of the planet on which you live. A very good thing, of course, but at the same time there is some conflict created if your slightly dream-like tendencies get in the way of your absolute need to see things through to their logical conclusion.

Nobody knows you better than you know yourself, or at least that's what the Aries qualities within you say, but that isn't always verified by some of the self-doubt that comes from the direction of the Fishes. As in all matters astrological, a position of balance has to be achieved in order to reconcile the differing qualities of your nature. In your case, this is best accomplished by being willing to stop and think once in a while and by refusing to allow your depth to be a problem.

Dealt with properly, the conjoining of Pisces and Aries can be a wondrous and joyful affair, a harmony of opposites that always makes you interesting to know. Your position in the world is naturally one of authority but at the same time you need to serve. That's why some people with this sort of mixture of astrological qualities would make such good administrators in a hospital, or in any position where the alternate astrological needs are well balanced. In the chocolate box of life you are certainly a 'soft centre'.

The Taurus Cusp – April 18th to April 20th

The merge from Aries to Taurus is much less well defined than the one at the other side of Aries, but it can be very useful to you all the same. Like the Pisces-influenced Aries you may be slightly more quiet than would be the case with the Ram taken alone and your thought processes are probably not quite as fast. But to compensate for this fact you don't rush into things quite as much and are willing to allow ideas to mature more fully.

Your sense of harmony and beauty is strong and you know, in a very definite way, exactly what you want. As a result your home will be distinctive but tasteful and it's a place where you need space to be alone sometimes, which the true Aries subject probably does not. You do not lack the confidence to make things look the way you want them, but you have a need to display these things to the world at large and sometimes even to talk about how good you are at decoration and design.

If anyone finds you pushy, it is probably because they don't really know what makes you tick. Although you are willing to mix with almost anyone, you are more inclined, at base, to have a few very close friends who stay at the forefront of your life for a long time. It is likely that you enjoy refined company and you wouldn't take kindly to the dark, the sordid, or the downright crude in life.

Things don't get you down as much as can sometimes be seen to be the case for Taurus when taken alone and you are rarely stumped for a progressive and practical idea when one is needed most. At all levels, your creative energy is evident and some of you even have the ability to make this into a business, since Aries offers the practical and administrative spark that Taurus can sometimes lack.

In matters of love, you are ardent and sincere, probably an idealist, and you know what you want in a partner. Whilst this is also true in the case of Taurus, you are different, because you are much more likely, not only to look, but also to say something about the way you feel.

Being naturally friendly you rarely go short of the right sort of help and support when it is most vital. Part of the reason for this lies in the fact that you are so willing to be the sounding-board for the concerns of your friends. All in all you can be very contented with your lot, but you never stop searching for something better all the same. At its best, this is one of the most progressive cuspal matches of them all.

ARIES AND ITS ASCENDANTS

The nature of every individual on the planet is composed of the rich variety of zodiac signs and planetary positions that were present at the time of their birth. Your Sun sign, which in your case is Aries, is one of the many factors when it comes to assessing the unique person you are. Probably the most important consideration, other than your Sun sign, is to establish the zodiac sign that was rising over the eastern horizon at the time that you were born. This is your Ascending or Rising sign. Most popular astrology fails to take account of the Ascendant, and yet its importance remains with you from the very moment of your birth, through every day of your life. The Ascendant is evident in the way you approach the world, and so, when meeting a person for the first time, it is this astrological influence that you are most likely to notice first. Our Ascending sign essentially represents what we appear to be, while our Sun sign is what we feel inside ourselves.

The Ascendant also has the potential for modifying our overall nature. For example, if you were born at a time of day when Aries was passing over the eastern horizon (this would be around the time of dawn) then you would be classed as a double Aries. As such you would typify this zodiac sign, both internally and in your dealings with others. However, if your Ascendant sign turned out to be a Water sign, such as Pisces, there would be a profound alteration of nature, away from the expected qualities of Aries.

One of the reasons that popular astrology often ignores the Ascendant is that it has always been rather difficult to establish. Old Moore has found a way to make this possible by devising an easy-to-use table, which you will find on page 158 of this book. Using this, you can establish your Ascendant sign at a glance. You will need to know your rough time of birth, then it is simply a case of following the instructions.

For those readers who have no idea of their time of birth it might be worth allowing a good friend, or perhaps your partner, to read through the section that follows this introduction. Someone who deals with you on a regular basis may easily discover your Ascending sign, even though you could have some difficulty establishing it for yourself. A good understanding of this component of your nature is essential if you want to be aware of that 'other person' who is responsible for the way you make contact with the world at large. Your Sun sign, Ascendant sign, and the other pointers in this book will, together, allow you a far better understanding of what makes you tick as an individual. Peeling back the different layers of your astrological make-up can be an enlightening experience, and the Ascendant may represent one of the most important layers of all.

Aries with Aries Ascendant

What you see is what you get with this combination. You typify the no-nonsense approach of Aries at its best. All the same this combination is quite daunting when viewed through the eyes of other, less dominant sorts of people. You tend to push your way though situations that would find others cowering in a corner and you are afraid of very little. With a determination to succeed that makes you a force to be reckoned with, you leave the world in no doubt as to your intentions and tend to be rather too brusque for your own good on occasions.

At heart you are kind and loving, able to offer assistance to the downtrodden and sad, and usually willing to take on board the cares of people who have a part to play in your life. No-one would doubt your sincerity, or your honesty, though you may utilise slightly less than orthodox ways of getting your own way on those occasions when you feel you have right on your side. You are a loving partner and a good parent, though where children are concerned you tend to be rather too protective. The trouble is that you know what a big, bad world it can be and probably feel that you are better equipped to deal with things than anyone else.

Aries with Taurus Ascendant

This is a much quieter combination, so much so that even experienced astrologers would be unlikely to recognise you as an Aries subject at all, unless of course they came to know you very well. Your approach to life tends to be quiet and considered and there is a great danger that you could suppress those feelings that others of your kind would be only too willing to verbalise. To compensate you are deeply creative and will think matters through much more readily than more dominant Aries types would be inclined to do. Reaching out towards the world, you are, nevertheless, somewhat locked inside yourself and can struggle to achieve the level of communication that you so desperately need. Frustration might easily follow, were it not for the fact that you possess a quiet determination that, to those in the know, is the clearest window through to your Aries soul.

The care for others is stronger here than with almost any other Aries type and you certainly demonstrate this at all levels. The fact is that you live a great percentage of your life in service to the people you take to, whilst at the same time being able to shut the door firmly in the face of people who irritate or anger you. You are deeply motivated towards family relationships.

Aries with Gemini Ascendant

A fairly jolly combination this, though by no means easy for others to come to terms with. You fly about from pillar to post and rarely stop long enough to take a breath. Admittedly this suits your own needs very well, but it can be a source of some disquiet to those around you, since they may not possess your energy or motivation. Those who know you well are deeply in awe of your capacity to keep going long after almost everyone else would have given up and gone home, though this quality is not always as wonderful as it sounds because it means that you put more pressure on your nervous system than just about any other astrological combination.

You need to be mindful of your nervous system, which responds to the erratic, mercurial quality of Gemini. Problems only really arise when the Aries part of you makes demands that the Gemini component finds difficult to deal with. There are paradoxes galore here and some of them need sorting out if you are ever fully to understand yourself, or are to be in a position when others know what makes you tick.

In relationships you might be a little fickle, but you are a real charmer and never stuck for the right words, no matter who you are dealing with. Your tenacity knows no bounds, though perhaps it should!

Aries with Cancer Ascendant

The main problem that you experience in life shows itself as a direct result of the meshing of these two very different zodiac signs. At heart Aries needs to dominate, whereas Cancer shows a desire to nurture. All too often the result can be a protective arm that is so strong that nobody could possibly get out from under it. Lighten your own load, and that of those you care for, by being willing to sit back and watch others please themselves a little. You might think that you know best, and your heart is clearly in the right place, but try to realise what life is like when someone is always on hand to tell you that they know better then you do.

But in a way this is a little severe, because you are fairly intuitive and your instincts would rarely lead you astray. Nobody could ask for a better partner or parent than you, though they might request a slightly less attentive one. In matters of work you are conscientious and are probably best suited to a job that means sorting out the kind of mess that humanity is so good at creating. You probably spend your spare time untangling balls of wool, though you are quite sporting too and could easily make the Olympics. Once there you would not win however, because you would be too concerned about all the other competitors.

Aries with Leo Ascendant

Here we come upon the first situation of Aries being allied with another Fire sign. This creates a character that could appear to be typically Aries at first sight and in many ways it is, though there are subtle differences that should not be ignored. Although you have the typical Aries ability to get things done, many of the tasks you do undertake will be for and on behalf of others. You can be proud, and on some occasions even haughty, and yet you are also regal in your bearing and honest to the point of absurdity. Nobody could doubt your sincerity and you have the soul of a poet combined with the courage of a lion.

All this is good, but it makes you rather difficult to approach, unless the person in question has first adopted a crouching and subservient attitude although you would not wish them to do so. It's simply that the impression you give and the motivation that underpins it are two quite different things. You are greatly respected and in the case of those individuals who know your real nature, you are also deeply loved. But life would be much simpler if you didn't always have to fight the wars that those around you are happy to start. Relaxation is a word that you don't really understand and you would do yourself a favour if you looked it up in a dictionary.

Aries with Virgo Ascendant

Virgo is steady and sure, though also fussy and stubborn. Aries is fast and determined, restless and active. It can already be seen that this is a rather strange meeting of characteristics and because Virgo is ruled by the capricious Mercury, the ultimate result will change from hour to hour and day to day. It isn't merely that others find it difficult to know where they are with you, they can't even understand what makes you tick. This will make you the subject of endless fascination and attention, at which you will be apparently surprised but inwardly pleased. If anyone ever really gets to know what goes on in that busy mind they may find the implications very difficult to deal with and it is a fact that only you would have the ability to live inside your crowded head.

As a partner and a parent you are second to none, though you tend to get on better with your children once they start to grow, since by this time you may be slightly less restricting to their own desires, which will often clash with your own on their behalf. You are capable of give and take and could certainly not be considered selfish, though your constant desire to get the best from everyone might occasionally be misconstrued.

Aries with Libra Ascendant

Libra has the tendency to bring out the best in any zodiac sign, and this is no exception when it comes together with Aries. You may, in fact, be the most comfortable of all Aries types, simply because Libra tempers some of your more assertive qualities and gives you the chance to balance out opposing forces, both inside yourself and in the world outside. You are fun to be with and make the staunchest friend possible. Although you are generally affable, few people would try to put one over on you, because they would quickly come to know how far you are willing to go before you let forth a string of invective that would shock those who previously underestimated your basic Aries traits.

Home and family are very dear to you, but you are more tolerant than some Aries types are inclined to be and you have a youthful zest for life that should stay with you no matter what age you manage to achieve. There is always something interesting to do and your mind is a constant stream of possibilities. This makes you very creative and you may also demonstrate a desire to look good at all times. You may not always be quite as confident as you appear to be, but few would guess the fact.

Aries with Scorpio Ascendant

The two very different faces of Mars come together in this potent, magnetic and quite awe-inspiring combination. Your natural inclination is towards secrecy and this fact, together with the natural attractions of the sensual Scorpio nature, makes you the object of great curiosity. This means that you will not go short of attention and should ensure that you are always being analysed by people who may never get to know you at all. At heart you prefer your own company, and yet life appears to find means to push you into the public gaze time and again. Most people with this combination ooze sex appeal and can use this fact as a stepping stone to personal success, yet without losing any integrity or loosening the cords of a deeply moralistic nature.

On those occasions when you do lose your temper, there isn't a character in the length and breadth of the zodiac who would have either the words or the courage to stand against the stream of invective that follows. On really rare occasions you might even scare yourself. As far as family members are concerned a simple look should be enough to show when you are not amused. Few people are left unmoved by your presence in their life.

Aries with Sagittarius Ascendant

What a lovely combination this can be, for the devil-may-care aspects of Sagittarius lighten the load of a sometimes too-serious Aries interior. Everything that glistens is not gold, though it's hard to convince you of the fact because, to mix metaphors, you can make a silk purse out of a sow's ear. Almost everyone loves you and in return you offer a friendship that is warm and protective, but not as demanding as sometimes tends to be the case with the Aries type. Relationships may be many and varied and there is often more than one major attachment in the life of those holding this combination. You will bring a breath of spring to any attachment, though you need to ensure that the person concerned is capable of keeping up with the hectic pace of your life.

It may appear from time to time that you are rather too trusting for your own good, though deep inside you are very astute and it seems that almost everything you undertake works out well in the end. This has nothing to do with native luck and is really down to the fact that you are much more calculating than might appear to be the case at first sight. As a parent you are protective yet offer sufficient room for self-expression.

Aries with Capricorn Ascendant

If ever anyone could be accused of setting off immediately, but slowly, it has to be you. These are very contradictory signs and the differences will express themselves in a variety of ways. One thing is certain, you have tremendous tenacity and will see a job through patiently from beginning to end, without tiring on the way, and ensuring that every detail is taken care of properly. This combination often bestows good health and a great capacity for continuity, particularly in terms of the length of life. You are certainly not as argumentative as the typical Aries, but you do know how to get your own way, which is just as well because you are usually thinking on behalf of everyone else and not just on your own account.

At home you can relax, which is a blessing for Aries, though in fact you seldom choose to do so because you always have some project or other on the go. You probably enjoy knocking down and rebuilding walls, though this is a practical tendency and not responsive to relationships, in which you are ardent and sincere. Impetuosity is as close to your heart as is the case for any type of Aries subject, though you certainly have the ability to appear patient and steady. But it's just a front, isn't it?

19

Aries with Aquarius Ascendant

The person standing on a soap box in the corner of the park, extolling the virtues of this or that, could quite easily be an Aries with an Aquarian Ascendant. You are certainly not averse to speaking your mind and you have plenty to talk about because you are the best social reformer and political animal of them all. Unorthodox in your approach, you have the ability to keep everyone guessing, except when it comes to getting your own way, for in this nobody doubts your natural abilities. You can put theories into practice very well and on the way you retain a sense of individuality that would shock more conservative types. It's true that a few people might find you a little difficult to approach and this is partly because you have an inner reserve and strength which is difficult for others to fathom.

In the world at large you take your place at the front, as any good Arian should, and yet you offer room for others to share your platform. You keep up with the latest innovations and treat family members as the genuine friends that you believe them to be. Care needs to be taken when picking a life partner, for you are an original, and not just anyone could match the peculiarities thrown up by this astrological combination.

Aries with Pisces Ascendant

Although not an easy combination to deal with, the Aries with a Piscean Ascendant does, nevertheless, bring something very special to the world in the way of natural understanding allied to practical assistance. It's true that you can sometimes be a dreamer, but there is nothing wrong with that as long as you have the ability to turn some of your wishes into reality, and this you are easily able to do, usually for the sake of those around you. Conversation comes easily to you, though you also possess a slightly wistful and poetic side to your nature, which is attractive to the many people who call you a friend. A natural entertainer, you bring a sense of the comic to the often serious qualities of Aries, though without losing the determination that typifies the sign.

In relationships you are ardent, sincere and supportive, with a strong social conscience that sometimes finds you fighting the battles of the less privileged members of society. Family is important to you and this is a combination that invariably leads to parenthood. Away from the cut and thrust of everyday life you relax more fully and think about matters more deeply than more typical Aries types might.

THE MOON AND THE PART IT PLAYS IN YOUR LIFE

In astrology the Moon is probably the single most important heavenly body after the Sun. Its unique position, as partner to the Earth on its journey around the solar system, means that the Moon appears to pass through the signs of the zodiac extremely quickly. The zodiac position of the Moon at the time of your birth plays a great part in personal character and is especially significant in the build-up of your emotional nature.

Sun Moon Cycles

The first lunar cycle deals with the part the position of the Moon plays relative to your Sun sign. I have made the fluctuations of this pattern easy for you to understand by means of a simple cyclic graph. It appears on the first page of each 'Your Month At A Glance', under the title 'Highs and Lows'. The graph displays the lunar cycle and you will soon learn to understand how its movements have a bearing on your level of energy and your abilities.

Your Own Moon Sign

Discovering the position of the Moon at the time of your birth has always been notoriously difficult because tracking the complex zodiac positions of the Moon is not easy. This process has been reduced to three simple stages with Old Moore's unique Lunar Tables. A breakdown of the Moon's zodiac positions can be found from page 25 onwards, so that once you know what your Moon Sign is, you can see what part this plays in the overall build-up of your personal character.

If you follow the instructions on the next page you will soon be able to work out exactly what zodiac sign the Moon occupied on the day that you were born and you can then go on to compare the reading for this position with those of your Sun sign and your Ascendant. It is partly the comparison between these three important positions that goes towards making you the unique individual you are.

HOW TO DISCOVER YOUR MOON SIGN

This is a three-stage process. You may need a pen and a piece of paper but if you follow the instructions below the process should only take a minute or so.

STAGE 1 First of all you need to know the Moon Age at the time of your birth. If you look at Moon Table 1, on page 23, you will find all the years between 1909 and 2007 down the left side. Find the year of your birth and then trace across to the right to the month of your birth. Where the two intersect you will find a number. This is the date of the New Moon in the month that you were born. You now need to count forward the number of days between the New Moon and your own birthday. For example, if the New Moon in the month of your birth was shown as being the 6th and you were born on the 20th, your Moon Age Day would be 14. If the New Moon in the month of your birth came after your birthday, you need to count forward from the New Moon in the previous month. If you were born in a Leap Year, remember to count the 29th February. You can tell if your birth year was a Leap Year if the last two digits can be divided by four. Whatever the result, jot this number down so that you do not forget it.

STAGE 2 Take a look at Moon Table 2 on page 24. Down the left hand column look for the date of your birth. Now trace across to the month of your birth. Where the two meet you will find a letter. Copy this letter down alongside your Moon Age Day.

STAGE 3 Moon Table 3 on page 24 will supply you with the zodiac sign the Moon occupied on the day of your birth. Look for your Moon Age Day down the left hand column and then for the letter you found in Stage 2. Where the two converge you will find a zodiac sign and this is the sign occupied by the Moon on the day that you were born.

Your Zodiac Moon Sign Explained

You will find a profile of all zodiac Moon Signs on pages 25 to 28, showing in yet another way how astrology helps to make you into the individual that you are. In each daily entry of the Astral Diary you can find the zodiac position of the Moon for every day of the year. This also allows you to discover your lunar birthdays. Since the Moon passes through all the signs of the zodiac in about a month, you can expect something like twelve lunar birthdays each year. At these times you are likely to be emotionally steady and able to make the sort of decisions that have real, lasting value.

MOON TABLE 1

YEAR	FEB	MAR	APR	YEAR	FEB	MAR	APR	YEAR	FEB	MAR	APR
1909	20	21	20	1942	15	16	15	1975	11	12	11
1910	9	11	9	1943	4	6	4	1976	29	30	29
1911	28	30	28	1944	24	24	22	1977	18	19	18
1912	17	19	18	1945	12	14	12	1978	7	9	7
1913	6	7	6	1946	2	3	2	1979	26	27	26
1914	24	26	24	1947	19	21	20	1980	15	16	15
1915	14	15	13	1948	9	11	9	1981	4	6	4
1916	3	5	3	1949	27	29	28	1982	23	24	23
1917	22	23	22	1950	16	18	17	1983	13	14	13
1918	11	12	11	1951	6	7	6	1984	1	2	1
1919	–	2/31	30	1952	25	25	24	1985	19	21	20
1920	19	20	18	1953	14	15	13	1986	9	10	9
1921	8	9	8	1954	3	5	3	1987	28	29	28
1922	26	28	27	1955	22	24	22	1988	17	18	16
1923	15	17	16	1956	11	12	11	1989	6	7	6
1924	5	5	4	1957	–	1/31	29	1990	25	26	25
1925	23	24	23	1958	18	20	19	1991	14	15	13
1926	12	14	12	1959	7	9	8	1992	3	4	3
1927	2	3	2	1960	26	27	26	1993	22	24	22
1928	19	21	20	1961	15	16	15	1994	10	12	11
1929	9	11	9	1962	5	6	5	1995	29	30	29
1930	28	30	28	1963	23	25	23	1996	18	19	18
1931	17	19	18	1964	13	14	12	1997	7	9	7
1932	6	7	6	1965	1	2	1	1998	26	27	26
1933	24	26	24	1966	19	21	20	1999	16	17	16
1934	14	15	13	1967	9	10	9	2000	5	6	4
1935	3	5	3	1968	28	29	28	2001	23	24	23
1936	22	23	21	1969	17	18	16	2002	12	13	12
1937	11	13	12	1970	6	7	6	2003	–	2	1
1938	–	2/31	30	1971	25	26	25	2004	20	21	19
1939	19	20	19	1972	14	15	13	2005	9	10	8
1940	8	9	7	1973	4	5	3	2006	28	29	27
1941	26	27	26	1974	22	24	22	2007	16	18	17

TABLE 2

DAY	MAR	APR
1	F	J
2	G	J
3	G	J
4	G	J
5	G	J
6	G	J
7	G	J
8	G	J
9	G	J
10	G	J
11	G	K
12	H	K
13	H	K
14	H	K
15	H	K
16	H	K
17	H	K
18	H	K
19	H	K
20	H	K
21	H	L
22	I	L
23	I	L
24	I	L
25	I	L
26	I	L
27	I	L
28	I	L
29	I	L
30	I	L
31	I	–

MOON TABLE 3

M/D	F	G	H	I	J	K	L
0	PI	PI	AR	AR	AR	TA	TA
1	PI	AR	AR	AR	TA	TA	TA
2	AR	AR	AR	TA	TA	TA	GE
3	AR	AR	TA	TA	TA	GE	GE
4	AR	TA	TA	GE	GE	GE	GE
5	TA	TA	GE	GE	GE	CA	CA
6	TA	GE	GE	GE	CA	CA	CA
7	GE	GE	GE	CA	CA	CA	LE
8	GE	GE	CA	CA	CA	LE	LE
9	CA	CA	CA	CA	LE	LE	VI
10	CA	CA	LE	LE	LE	VI	VI
11	CA	LE	LE	LE	VI	VI	VI
12	LE	LE	LE	VI	VI	VI	LI
13	LE	LE	VI	VI	VI	LI	LI
14	VI	VI	VI	LI	LI	LI	LI
15	VI	VI	LI	LI	LI	SC	SC
16	VI	LI	LI	LI	SC	SC	SC
17	LI	LI	LI	SC	SC	SC	SA
18	LI	LI	SC	SC	SC	SA	SA
19	LI	SC	SC	SC	SA	SA	SA
20	SC	SC	SA	SA	SA	CP	CP
21	SC	SA	SA	SA	CP	CP	CP
22	SC	SA	SA	CP	CP	CP	AQ
23	SA	SA	CP	CP	CP	AQ	AQ
24	SA	CP	CP	CP	AQ	AQ	AQ
25	CP	CP	AQ	AQ	AQ	PI	PI
26	CP	AQ	AQ	AQ	PI	PI	PI
27	AQ	AQ	AQ	PI	PI	PI	AR
28	AQ	AQ	PI	PI	PI	AR	AR
29	AQ	PI	PI	PI	AR	AR	AR

AR = Aries, TA = Taurus, GE = Gemini, CA = Cancer, LE = Leo, VI = Virgo, LI = Libra, SC = Scorpio, SA = Sagittarius, CP = Capricorn, AQ = Aquarius, PI = Pisces

MOON SIGNS

Moon in Aries

You have a strong imagination, courage, determination and a desire to do things in your own way and forge your own path through life.

Originality is a key attribute; you are seldom stuck for ideas although your mind is changeable and you could take the time to focus on individual tasks. Often quick-tempered, you take orders from few people and live life at a fast pace. Avoid health problems by taking regular time out for rest and relaxation.

Emotionally, it is important that you talk to those you are closest to and work out your true feelings. Once you discover that people are there to help, there is less necessity for you to do everything yourself.

Moon in Taurus

The Moon in Taurus gives you a courteous and friendly manner, which means you are likely to have many friends.

The good things in life mean a lot to you, as Taurus is an Earth sign that delights in experiences which please the senses. Hence you are probably a lover of good food and drink, which may in turn mean you need to keep an eye on the bathroom scales, especially as looking good is also important to you.

Emotionally you are fairly stable and you stick by your own standards. Taureans do not respond well to change. Intuition also plays an important part in your life.

Moon in Gemini

You have a warm-hearted character, sympathetic and eager to help others. At times reserved, you can also be articulate and chatty: this is part of the paradox of Gemini, which always brings duplicity to the nature. You are interested in current affairs, have a good intellect, and are good company and likely to have many friends. Most of your friends have a high opinion of you and would be ready to defend you should the need arise. However, this is usually unnecessary, as you are quite capable of defending yourself in any verbal confrontation.

Travel is important to your inquisitive mind and you find intellectual stimulus in mixing with people from different cultures. You also gain much from reading, writing and the arts but you do need plenty of rest and relaxation in order to avoid fatigue.

Moon in Cancer

The Moon in Cancer at the time of birth is a fortunate position as Cancer is the Moon's natural home. This means that the qualities of compassion and understanding given by the Moon are especially enhanced in your nature, and you are friendly and sociable and cope well with emotional pressures. You cherish home and family life, and happily do the domestic tasks. Your surroundings are important to you and you hate squalor and filth. You are likely to have a love of music and poetry.

Your basic character, although at times changeable like the Moon itself, depends on symmetry. You aim to make your surroundings comfortable and harmonious, for yourself and those close to you.

Moon in Leo

The best qualities of the Moon and Leo come together to make you warm-hearted, fair, ambitious and self-confident. With good organisational abilities, you invariably rise to a position of responsibility in your chosen career. This is fortunate as you don't enjoy being an 'also-ran' and would rather be an important part of a small organisation than a menial in a large one.

You should be lucky in love, and happy, provided you put in the effort to make a comfortable home for yourself and those close to you. It is likely that you will have a love of pleasure, sport, music and literature. Life brings you many rewards, most of them as a direct result of your own efforts, although you may be luckier than average and ready to make the best of any situation.

Moon in Virgo

You are endowed with good mental abilities and a keen receptive memory, but you are never ostentatious or pretentious. Naturally quite reserved, you still have many friends, especially of the opposite sex. Marital relationships must be discussed carefully and worked at so that they remain harmonious, as personal attachments can be a problem if you do not give them your full attention.

Talented and persevering, you possess artistic qualities and are a good homemaker. Earning your honours through genuine merit, you work long and hard towards your objectives but show little pride in your achievements. Many short journeys will be undertaken in your life.

Moon in Libra

With the Moon in Libra you are naturally popular and make friends easily. People like you, probably more than you realise, you bring fun to a party and are a natural diplomat. For all its good points, Libra is not the most stable of astrological signs and, as a result, your emotions can be a little unstable too. Therefore, although the Moon in Libra is said to be good for love and marriage, your Sun sign and Rising sign will have an important effect on your emotional and loving qualities.

You must remember to relate to others in your decision-making. Co-operation is crucial because Libra represents the 'balance' of life that can only be achieved through harmonious relationships. Conformity is not easy for you because Libra, an Air sign, likes its independence.

Moon in Scorpio

Some people might call you pushy. In fact, all you really want to do is to live life to the full and protect yourself and your family from the pressures of life. Take care to avoid giving the impression of being sarcastic or impulsive and use your energies wisely and constructively.

You have great courage and you invariably achieve your goals by force of personality and sheer effort. You are fond of mystery and are good at predicting the outcome of situations and events. Travel experiences can be beneficial to you.

You may experience problems if you do not take time to examine your motives in a relationship, and also if you allow jealousy, always a feature of Scorpio, to cloud your judgement.

Moon in Sagittarius

The Moon in Sagittarius helps to make you a generous individual with humanitarian qualities and a kind heart. Restlessness may be intrinsic as your mind is seldom still. Perhaps because of this, you have a need for change that could lead you to several major moves during your adult life. You are not afraid to stand your ground when you know your judgement is right, you speak directly and have good intuition.

At work you are quick, efficient and versatile and so you make an ideal employee. You need work to be intellectually demanding and do not enjoy tedious routines.

In relationships, you anger quickly if faced with stupidity or deception, though you are just as quick to forgive and forget. Emotionally, there are times when your heart rules your head.

Moon in Capricorn

The Moon in Capricorn makes you popular and likely to come into the public eye in some way. The watery Moon is not entirely comfortable in the Earth sign of Capricorn and this may lead to some difficulties in the early years of life. An initial lack of creative ability and indecision must be overcome before the true qualities of patience and perseverance inherent in Capricorn can show through.

You have good administrative ability and are a capable worker, and if you are careful you can accumulate wealth. But you must be cautious and take professional advice in partnerships, as you are open to deception. You may be interested in social or welfare work, which suit your organisational skills and sympathy for others.

Moon in Aquarius

The Moon in Aquarius makes you an active and agreeable person with a friendly, easy-going nature. Sympathetic to the needs of others, you flourish in a laid-back atmosphere. You are broad-minded, fair and open to suggestion, although sometimes you have an unconventional quality which others can find hard to understand.

You are interested in the strange and curious, and in old articles and places. You enjoy trips to these places and gain much from them. Political, scientific and educational work interests you and you might choose a career in science or technology.

Money-wise, you make gains through innovation and concentration and Lunar Aquarians often tackle more than one job at a time. In love you are kind and honest.

Moon in Pisces

You have a kind, sympathetic nature, somewhat retiring at times, but you always take account of others' feelings and help when you can.

Personal relationships may be problematic, but as life goes on you can learn from your experiences and develop a better understanding of yourself and the world around you.

You have a fondness for travel, appreciate beauty and harmony and hate disorder and strife. You may be fond of literature and would make a good writer or speaker yourself. You have a creative imagination and may come across as an incurable romantic. You have strong intuition, maybe bordering on a mediumistic quality, which sets you apart from the mass. You may not be rich in cash terms, but your personal gifts are worth more than gold.

ARIES IN LOVE

Discover how compatible in love you are with people from the same and other signs of the zodiac. Five stars equals a match made in heaven!

Aries meets Aries

This could be be an all-or-nothing pairing. Both parties are from a dominant sign, so someone will have to be flexible in order to maintain personal harmony. Both know what they want out of life, and may have trouble overcoming any obstacles a relationship creates. This is a good physical pairing, with a chemistry that few other matches enjoy to the same level. Attitude is everything, but at least there is a mutual admiration that makes gazing at your partner like looking in the mirror. Star rating: ****

Aries meets Taurus

This is a match that has been known to work very well. Aries brings dynamism and ambition, while Taurus has the patience to see things through logically. Such complementary views work equally well in a relationship or in the office. There is mutual respect, but sometimes a lack of total understanding. The romantic needs of each are quite different, but both are still fulfilled. They can live easily in domestic harmony which is very important but, interestingly, Aries may be the loser in battles of will. Star rating: ***

Aries meets Gemini

Don't expect peace and harmony with this combination, although what comes along instead might make up for any disagreements. Gemini has a very fertile imagination, while Aries has the tenacity to make reality from fantasy. Combined, they have a sizzling relationship. There are times when both parties could explode with indignation and something has to give. But even if there are clashes, making them up will always be most enjoyable! Mutual financial success is likely in this match. Star rating: ****

Aries meets Cancer

A potentially one-sided pairing, it often appears that the Cancerian is brow-beaten by the far more dominant Arian. So much depends on the patience of the Cancerian individual, because if good psychology is present – who knows? But beware, Aries, you may find your partner too passive, and constantly having to take the lead can be wearing – even for you. A prolonged trial period would be advantageous, as the match could easily go either way. When it does work, though, this relationship is usually contented. Star rating: ***

Aries meets Leo

Stand by for action and make sure the house is sound-proof. Leo is a lofty idealist and there is always likely to be friction when two Fire signs meet. To compensate, there is much mutual admiration, together with a desire to please. Where there are shared incentives, the prognosis is good but it's important not to let little irritations blow up. Both signs want to have their own way and this is a sure cause of trouble. There might not be much patience here, but there is plenty of action. Star rating: *****

Aries meets Virgo

Neither of these signs really understands the other, and that could easily lead to a clash. Virgo is so pedantic, which will drive Aries up the wall, while Aries always wants to be moving on to the next objective, before Virgo is even settled with the last one. It will take time for these two to get to know each other, but this is a great business matching. If a personal relationship is seen in these terms then the prognosis can be good, but on the whole, this is not an inspiring match. Star rating: ***

Aries meets Libra

These signs are zodiac opposites which means a make-or-break situation. The match will either be a great success or a dismal failure. Why? Well Aries finds it difficult to understand the flighty Air-sign tendencies of Libra, whilst the natural balance of Libra contradicts the unorthodox Arian methods. Any flexibility will come from Libra, which may mean that things work out for a while, but Libra only has so much patience and it may eventually run out. In the end, Aries may be just too bossy for an independent but sensitive sign like Libra. Star rating: **

Aries meets Scorpio

There can be great affection here, even if the two zodiac signs are so very different. The common link is the planet Mars, which plays a part in both these natures. Although Aries is, outwardly, the most dominant, Scorpio people are among the most powerful to be found anywhere. This quiet determination is respected by Aries. Aries will satisfy the passionate side of Scorpio, particularly with instruction from Scorpio. There are mysteries here which will add spice to life. The few arguments that do occur are likely to be awe-inspiring. Star rating: ****

Aries meets Sagittarius

This can be one of the most favourable matches of them all. Both Aries and Sagittarius are Fire signs, which often leads to clashes of will, but this pair find a mutual understanding. Sagittarius helps Aries to develop a better sense of humour, while Aries teaches the Archer about consistency on the road to success. Some patience is called for on both sides, but these people have a natural liking for each other. Add this to growing love and you have a long-lasting combination that is hard to beat. Star rating: *****

Aries meets Capricorn

Capricorn works conscientiously to achieve its objectives and so can be the perfect companion for Aries. The Ram knows how to achieve but not how to consolidate, so the two signs have a great deal to offer one another practically. There may not be fireworks and it's sometimes doubtful how well they know each other, but it may not matter. Aries is outwardly hot but inwardly cool, whilst Capricorn can appear low key but be a furnace underneath. Such a pairing can gradually find contentment, though both parties may wonder how this is so. Star rating: ****

Aries meets Aquarius

Aquarius is an Air sign, and Air and Fire often work well together, but perhaps not in the case of Aries and Aquarius. The average Aquarian lives in what the Ram sees as a fantasy world, so without a sufficiently good meeting of minds, compromise may be lacking. Of course, almost anything is possible, and the dominant side of Aries could be trained by the devil-may-care attitude of Aquarius. There are meeting points but they are difficult to establish. However, given sufficient time and an open mind on both sides, a degree of happiness is possible. Star rating: **

Aries meets Pisces

Still waters run deep, and they don't come much deeper than Pisces. Although these signs share the same quadrant of the zodiac, they have little in common. Pisces is a dreamer, a romantic idealist with steady and spiritual goals. Aries needs to be on the move, and has very different ideals. It's hard to see how a relationship could develop because the outlook on life is so different but, with patience, especially from Aries, there is a chance that things might work out. Pisces needs incentive, and Aries may be the sign to offer it. Star rating: **

VENUS:
THE PLANET OF LOVE

If you look up at the sky around sunset or sunrise you will often see Venus in close attendance to the Sun. It is arguably one of the most beautiful sights of all and there is little wonder that historically it became associated with the goddess of love. But although Venus does play an important part in the way you view love and in the way others see you romantically, this is only one of the spheres of influence that it enjoys in your overall character.

Venus has a part to play in the more cultured side of your life and has much to do with your appreciation of art, literature, music and general creativity. Even the way you look is responsive to the part of the zodiac that Venus occupied at the start of your life, though this fact is also down to your Sun sign and Ascending sign. If, at the time you were born, Venus occupied one of the more gregarious zodiac signs, you will be more likely to wear your heart on your sleeve, as well as to be more attracted to entertainment, social gatherings and good company. If on the other hand Venus occupied a quiet zodiac sign at the time of your birth, you would tend to be more retiring and less willing to shine in public situations.

It's good to know what part the planet Venus plays in your life for it can have a great bearing on the way you appear to the rest of the world and since we all have to mix with others, you can learn to make the very best of what Venus has to offer you.

One of the great complications in the past has always been trying to establish exactly what zodiac position Venus enjoyed when you were born because the planet is notoriously difficult to track. However, I have solved that problem by creating a table that is exclusive to your Sun sign, which you will find on the following page.

Establishing your Venus sign could not be easier. Just look up the year of your birth on the page opposite and you will see a sign of the zodiac. This was the sign that Venus occupied in the period covered by your sign in that year. If Venus occupied more than one sign during the period, this is indicated by the date on which the sign changed, and the name of the new sign. For instance, if you were born in 1950, Venus was in Aquarius until the 7th April, after which time it was in Pisces. If you were born before 7th April your Venus sign is Aquarius, if you were born on or after 7th April, your Venus sign is Pisces. Once you have established the position of Venus at the time of your birth, you can then look in the pages which follow to see how this has a bearing on your life as a whole.

VENUS: THE PLANET OF LOVE

1909 PISCES / 29.3 ARIES
1910 AQUARIUS / 5.4 PISCES
1911 ARIES / 25.3 TAURUS
1912 PISCES / 14.4 ARIES
1913 TAURUS
1914 ARIES / 14.4 TAURUS
1915 AQUARIUS / 1.4 PISCES
1916 TAURUS / 8.4 GEMINI
1917 PISCES / 28.3 ARIES
1918 AQUARIUS / 5.4 PISCES
1919 ARIES / 24.3 TAURUS
1920 PISCES / 14.4 ARIES
1921 TAURUS
1922 ARIES / 13.4 TAURUS
1923 AQUARIUS / 1.4 PISCES
1924 TAURUS / 6.4 GEMINI
1925 PISCES / 28.3 ARIES
1926 AQUARIUS / 6.4 PISCES
1927 ARIES / 24.3 TAURUS
1928 PISCES / 13.4 ARIES
1929 TAURUS / 20.4 ARIES
1930 ARIES / 13.4 TAURUS
1931 AQUARIUS / 31.3 PISCES
1932 TAURUS / 6.4 GEMINI
1933 PISCES / 27.3 ARIES
1934 AQUARIUS / 6.4 PISCES
1935 ARIES / 23.3 TAURUS
1936 PISCES / 13.4 ARIES
1937 TAURUS / 14.4 ARIES
1938 ARIES / 12.4 TAURUS
1939 AQUARIUS / 31.3 PISCES
1940 TAURUS / 5.4 GEMINI
1941 PISCES / 26.3 ARIES /
    20.4 TAURUS
1942 AQUARIUS / 7.4 PISCES
1943 ARIES / 23.3 TAURUS
1944 PISCES / 12.4 ARIES
1945 TAURUS / 8.4 ARIES
1946 ARIES / 12.4 TAURUS
1947 AQUARIUS / 30.3 PISCES
1948 TAURUS / 5.4 GEMINI
1949 PISCES / 25.3 ARIES /
    20.4 TAURUS
1950 AQUARIUS / 7.4 PISCES
1951 ARIES / 22.3 TAURUS
1952 PISCES / 12.4 ARIES
1953 TAURUS / 1.4 ARIES
1954 ARIES / 11.4 TAURUS
1955 AQUARIUS / 30.3 PISCES
1956 TAURUS / 4.4 GEMINI
1957 PISCES / 25.3 ARIES /
    19.4 TAURUS
1958 AQUARIUS / 8.4 PISCES
1959 ARIES / 22.3 TAURUS

1960 PISCES / 11.4 ARIES
1961 ARIES
1962 ARIES / 11.4 TAURUS
1963 AQUARIUS / 29.3 PISCES
1964 TAURUS / 4.4 GEMINI
1965 PISCES / 24.3 ARIES /
    19.4 TAURUS
1966 AQUARIUS / 8.4 PISCES
1967 TAURUS / 20.4 GEMINI
1968 PISCES / 10.4 ARIES
1969 ARIES
1970 ARIES / 10.4 TAURUS
1971 AQUARIUS / 29.3 PISCES
1972 TAURUS / 3.4 GEMINI
1973 PISCES / 24.3 ARIES /
    18.4 TAURUS
1974 AQUARIUS / 8.4 PISCES
1975 TAURUS / 19.4 GEMINI
1976 PISCES / 10.4 ARIES
1977 ARIES
1978 ARIES / 10.4 TAURUS
1979 AQUARIUS / 28.3 PISCES
1980 TAURUS / 3.4 GEMINI
1981 PISCES / 23.3 ARIES /
    18.4 TAURUS
1982 AQUARIUS / 9.4 PISCES
1983 TAURUS / 19.4 GEMINI
1984 PISCES / 9.4 ARIES
1985 ARIES
1986 ARIES / 9.4 TAURUS
1987 AQUARIUS / 28.3 PISCES
1988 TAURUS / 2.4 GEMINI
1989 PISCES / 23.3 ARIES /
    17.4 TAURUS
1990 AQUARIUS / 9.4 PISCES
1991 TAURUS / 18.4 GEMINI
1992 PISCES / 9.4 ARIES
1993 ARIES
1994 ARIES / 9.4 TAURUS
1995 AQUARIUS / 27.3 PISCES
1996 TAURUS / 2.4 GEMINI
1997 PISCES / 22.3 ARIES /
    17.4 TAURUS
1998 AQUARIUS / 9.4 PISCES
1999 TAURUS / 18.4 GEMINI
2000 PISCES / 9.4 ARIES
2001 ARIES
2002 ARIES / 7.4 TAURUS
2003 AQUARIUS / 27.3 PISCES
2004 TAURUS / 1.4 GEMINI
2005 PISCES/22.3 ARIES
2006 AQUARIUS/7.4 PISCES
2007 TAURUS/16.4 GEMINI

33

VENUS THROUGH THE ZODIAC SIGNS

Venus in Aries

Amongst other things, the position of Venus in Aries indicates a fondness for travel, music and all creative pursuits. Your nature tends to be affectionate and you would try not to create confusion or difficulty for others if it could be avoided. Many people with this planetary position have a great love of the theatre, and mental stimulation is of the greatest importance. Early romantic attachments are common with Venus in Aries, so it is very important to establish a genuine sense of romantic continuity. Early marriage is not recommended, especially if it is based on sympathy. You may give your heart a little too readily on occasions.

Venus in Taurus

You are capable of very deep feelings and your emotions tend to last for a very long time. This makes you a trusting partner and lover, whose constancy is second to none. In life you are precise and careful and always try to do things the right way. Although this means an ordered life, which you are comfortable with, it can also lead you to be rather too fussy for your own good. Despite your pleasant nature, you are very fixed in your opinions and quite able to speak your mind. Others are attracted to you and historical astrologers always quoted this position of Venus as being very fortunate in terms of marriage. However, if you find yourself involved in a failed relationship, it could take you a long time to trust again.

Venus in Gemini

As with all associations related to Gemini, you tend to be quite versatile, anxious for change and intelligent in your dealings with the world at large. You may gain money from more than one source but you are equally good at spending it. There is an inference here that you are a good communicator, via either the written or the spoken word, and you love to be in the company of interesting people. Always on the look-out for culture, you may also be very fond of music, and love to indulge the curious and cultured side of your nature. In romance you tend to have more than one relationship and could find yourself associated with someone who has previously been a friend or even a distant relative.

Venus in Cancer

You often stay close to home because you are very fond of family and enjoy many of your most treasured moments when you are with those you love. Being naturally sympathetic, you will always do anything you can to support those around you, even people you hardly know at all. This charitable side of your nature is your most noticeable trait and is one of the reasons why others are naturally so fond of you. Being receptive and in some cases even psychic, you can see through to the soul of most of those with whom you come into contact. You may not commence too many romantic attachments but when you do give your heart, it tends to be unconditionally.

Venus in Leo

It must become quickly obvious to almost anyone you meet that you are kind, sympathetic and yet determined enough to stand up for anyone or anything that is truly important to you. Bright and sunny, you warm the world with your natural enthusiasm and would rarely do anything to hurt those around you, or at least not intentionally. In romance you are ardent and sincere, though some may find your style just a little overpowering. Gains come through your contacts with other people and this could be especially true with regard to romance, for love and money often come hand in hand for those who were born with Venus in Leo. People claim to understand you, though you are more complex than you seem.

Venus in Virgo

Your nature could well be fairly quiet no matter what your Sun sign might be, though this fact often manifests itself as an inner peace and would not prevent you from being basically sociable. Some delays and even the odd disappointment in love cannot be ruled out with this planetary position, though it's a fact that you will usually find the happiness you look for in the end. Catapulting yourself into romantic entanglements that you know to be rather ill-advised is not sensible, and it would be better to wait before you committed yourself exclusively to any one person. It is the essence of your nature to serve the world at large and through doing so it is possible that you will attract money at some stage in your life.

Venus in Libra

Venus is very comfortable in Libra and bestows upon those people who have this planetary position a particular sort of kindness that is easy to recognise. This is a very good position for all sorts of friendships and also for romantic attachments that usually bring much joy into your life. Few individuals with Venus in Libra would avoid marriage and since you are capable of great depths of love, it is likely that you will find a contented personal life. You like to mix with people of integrity and intelligence but don't take kindly to scruffy surroundings or work that means getting your hands too dirty. Careful speculation, good business dealings and money through marriage all seem fairly likely.

Venus in Scorpio

You are quite open and tend to spend money quite freely, even on those occasions when you don't have very much. Although your intentions are always good, there are times when you get yourself in to the odd scrape and this can be particularly true when it comes to romance, which you may come to late or from a rather unexpected direction. Certainly you have the power to be happy and to make others contented on the way, but you find the odd stumbling block on your journey through life and it could seem that you have to work harder than those around you. As a result of this, you gain a much deeper understanding of the true value of personal happiness than many people ever do, and are likely to achieve true contentment in the end.

Venus in Sagittarius

You are lighthearted, cheerful and always able to see the funny side of any situation. These facts enhance your popularity, which is especially high with members of the opposite sex. You should never have to look too far to find romantic interest in your life, though it is just possible that you might be too willing to commit yourself before you are certain that the person in question is right for you. Part of the problem here extends to other areas of life too. The fact is that you like variety in everything and so can tire of situations that fail to offer it. All the same, if you choose wisely and learn to understand your restless side, then great happiness can be yours.

Venus in Capricorn

The most notable trait that comes from Venus in this position is that it makes you trustworthy and able to take on all sorts of responsibilities in life. People are instinctively fond of you and love you all the more because you are always ready to help those who are in any form of need. Social and business popularity can be yours and there is a magnetic quality to your nature that is particularly attractive in a romantic sense. Anyone who wants a partner for a lover, a spouse and a good friend too would almost certainly look in your direction. Constancy is the hallmark of your nature and unfaithfulness would go right against the grain. You might sometimes be a little too trusting.

Venus in Aquarius

This location of Venus offers a fondness for travel and a desire to try out something new at every possible opportunity. You are extremely easy to get along with and tend to have many friends from varied backgrounds, classes and inclinations. You like to live a distinct sort of life and gain a great deal from moving about, both in a career sense and with regard to your home. It is not out of the question that you could form a romantic attachment to someone who comes from far away or be attracted to a person of a distinctly artistic and original nature. What you cannot stand is jealousy, for you have friends of both sexes and would want to keep things that way.

Venus in Pisces

The first thing people tend to notice about you is your wonderful, warm smile. Being very charitable by nature you will do anything to help others, even if you don't know them well. Much of your life may be spent sorting out situations for other people, but it is very important to feel that you are living for yourself too. In the main, you remain cheerful, and tend to be quite attractive to members of the opposite sex. Where romantic attachments are concerned, you could be drawn to people who are significantly older or younger than yourself or to someone with a unique career or point of view. It might be best for you to avoid marrying whilst you are still very young.

THE ASTRAL DIARY
HOW THE DIAGRAMS WORK

Through the picture diagrams in the Astral Diary I want to help you to plot your year. With them you can see where the positive and negative aspects will be found in each month. To make the most of them, all you have to do is remember where and when!

Let me show you how they work ...

THE MONTH AT A GLANCE

Just as there are twelve separate zodiac signs, so astrologers believe that each sign has twelve separate aspects to life. Each of the twelve segments relates to a different personal aspect. I list them all every month so that their meanings are always clear.

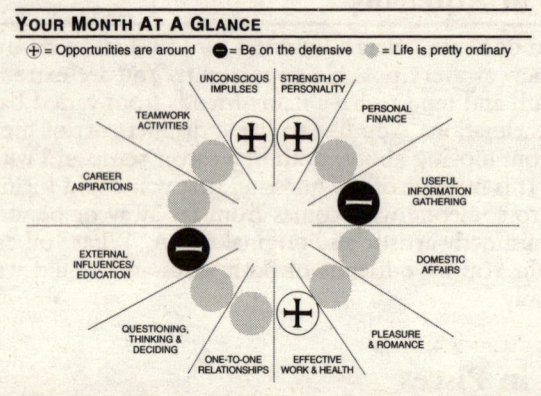

YOUR MONTH AT A GLANCE

⊕ = Opportunities are around   ⊖ = Be on the defensive   ● = Life is pretty ordinary

- UNCONSCIOUS IMPULSES
- STRENGTH OF PERSONALITY
- TEAMWORK ACTIVITIES
- PERSONAL FINANCE
- CAREER ASPIRATIONS
- USEFUL INFORMATION GATHERING
- EXTERNAL INFLUENCES/EDUCATION
- DOMESTIC AFFAIRS
- QUESTIONING, THINKING & DECIDING
- PLEASURE & ROMANCE
- ONE-TO-ONE RELATIONSHIPS
- EFFECTIVE WORK & HEALTH

I have designed this chart to show you how and when these twelve different aspects are being influenced throughout the year. When there is a shaded circle, nothing out of the ordinary is to be expected. However, when a circle turns white with a plus sign, the influence is positive. Where the circle is black with a minus sign, it is a negative.

YOUR ENERGY RHYTHM CHART

On the opposite page is a picture diagram in which I am linking your zodiac group to the rhythm of the Moon. In doing this I have calculated when you will be gaining strength from its influence and equally when you may be weakened by it.

If you think of yourself as being like the tides of the ocean then you may understand how your own energies must also rise and fall. And if you understand how it works and when it is working, then you can better organise your activities to achieve more and get things done more easily.

YOUR ENERGY RHYTHM CHART

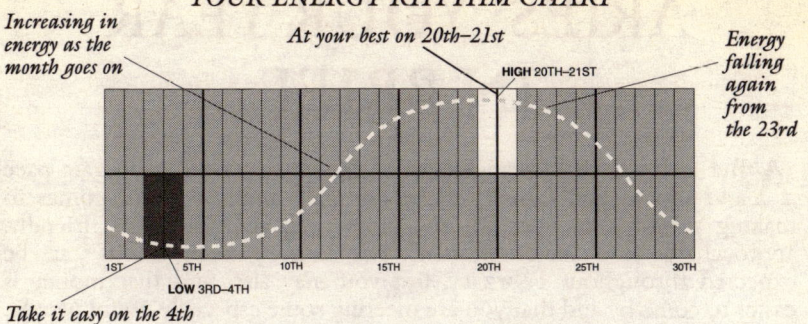

Increasing in energy as the month goes on

At your best on 20th–21st

HIGH 20TH–21ST

Energy falling again from the 23rd

1ST　5TH　10TH　15TH　20TH　25TH　30TH

LOW 3RD–4TH

Take it easy on the 4th

MOVING PICTURE SCREEN
Love, money, career and vitality measured every week

The diagram at the end of each week is designed to be informative and fun. The arrows move up and down the scale to give you an idea of the strength of your opportunities in each area. If LOVE stands at plus 4, then get out and put yourself about because things are going your way in romance! The further down the arrow goes, the weaker the opportunities. Do note that the diagram is an overall view of your astrological aspects and therefore reflects a trend which may not concur with every day in that cycle.

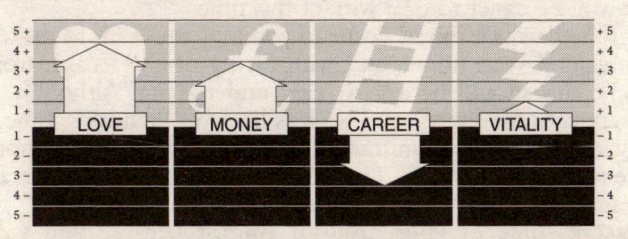

| LOVE | MONEY | CAREER | VITALITY |

AND FINALLY:

am ....
pm ....

The two lines that are left blank in each daily entry of the Astral Diary are for your own personal use. You may find them ideal for keeping a check on birthdays or appointments, though it could be an idea to make notes from the astrological trends and diagrams a few weeks in advance. Some of the lines are marked with a key, which indicates the working of astrological cycles in your life. Look out for them each week as they are the best days to take action or make decisions. The daily text tells you which area of your life to focus on.

☿ = Mercury is retrograde on that day.

ARIES: YOUR YEAR IN BRIEF

After a slower than average start to the year you will soon gain pace and should find January to be especially useful when it comes to making progress at work. At the same time you should be friendly, approachable and uncomplicated. The same general trends can be expected throughout February, but you may also find that money is easier to come by and that you are meeting some especially useful people. By the time the spring arrives you should be making significant progress and will discover something to your advantage during the first part of March. Things may then slow just a little, though there will be gains associated with love and romance and new friends on the horizon.

It is most likely at the start of April that you really begin to come alive. This is always a good time of year for you, and there are advantages to be gained from simply being in the right place at the best possible time. Rely on your intuition and continue to do so during May, which brings personal advantages, together with the possibility of advancement at work. This could be the first month of the year during which you look seriously at the possibility of travel, and it also appears that money matters will be easier to deal with at this time.

As June dawns it might occur to you that you want to make changes in and around your home, and with plenty of enthusiasm from family members, this should be a fairly easy undertaking. Although you have shown concern for those you love it is likely to be during June that you feel a greater family commitment, as well as experiencing another very positive romantic interlude. The following month of July increases these trends and also finds you anxious for change and diversity.

Reserve some of your cash for August because you will almost certainly need it. Travel is uppermost in your mind, as will be further changes to the homestead. The end of the month should be especially appealing in a social sense. September and October could be slightly quieter but they still have their benefits to offer and you will be able to use this time to look ahead quite successfully.

As the year draws to its close you will be more contemplative and establish a deeper understanding of exactly what it is you are looking for. A little restlessness soon passes, leaving you fairly content with your lot. November is practically busy, though during December much more of your time than usual is likely to be given to the festive season and to the needs of loved ones around this period. You exit the year feeling happy with your lot and should be fairly content with the overall progress of one of the most balanced years you have experienced for some time.

January 2007

YOUR MONTH AT A GLANCE

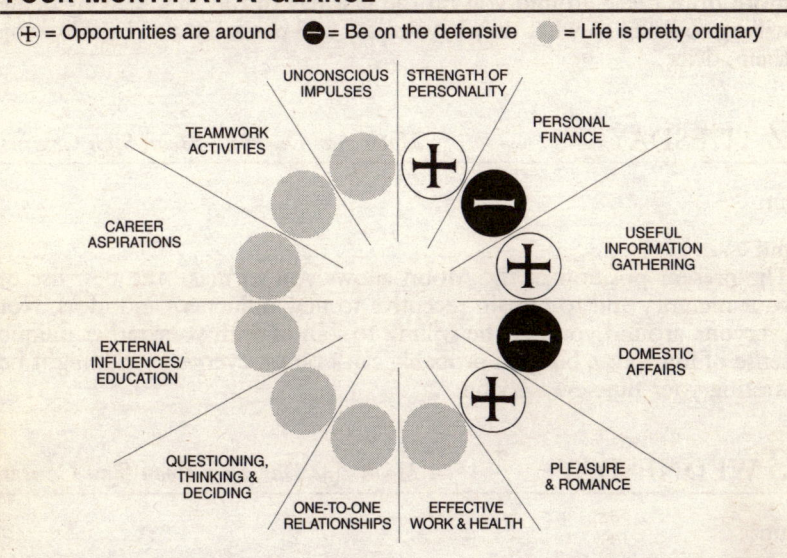

⊕ = Opportunities are around   ⊖ = Be on the defensive   ● = Life is pretty ordinary

- UNCONSCIOUS IMPULSES
- STRENGTH OF PERSONALITY ⊕
- TEAMWORK ACTIVITIES
- PERSONAL FINANCE ⊖
- CAREER ASPIRATIONS
- USEFUL INFORMATION GATHERING ⊕
- EXTERNAL INFLUENCES/EDUCATION
- DOMESTIC AFFAIRS ⊖
- QUESTIONING, THINKING & DECIDING
- PLEASURE & ROMANCE ⊕
- ONE-TO-ONE RELATIONSHIPS
- EFFECTIVE WORK & HEALTH

JANUARY HIGHS AND LOWS

Here I show you how the rhythms of the Moon will affect you this month. Like the tide, your energies and abilities will rise and fall with its pattern. When it is above the centre line, go for it, when it is below, you should be resting.

HIGH 24TH–25TH

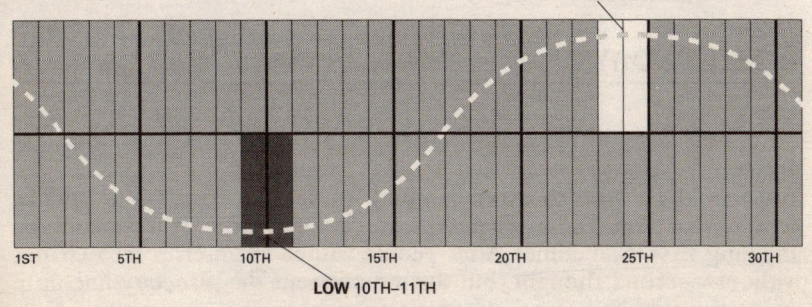

LOW 10TH–11TH

41

1 MONDAY   *Moon Age Day 13   Moon Sign Gemini*

am ....

pm ....
Although scoring points over others can lift your ego today, in reality you may be better off remaining a little humble. You can probably get far more from those around you on the first day of this new year by being willing to listen to what they have to say and probably also by following their advice.

2 TUESDAY   *Moon Age Day 14   Moon Sign Gemini*

am ....

pm ....
The present position of the Moon allows you to make the best use of your memory and to remain receptive to new influences and ideas. Not everyone around you may be willing to join in with your rather unique sense of fun today, but you probably can't please everyone and might be wasting your time even trying.

3 WEDNESDAY   *Moon Age Day 15   Moon Sign Cancer*

am ....

pm ....
For some Aries people this can be a time of transition as far as your career is concerned. Maybe you see the start of the year as a time during which you want to make significant changes, or it could be that alterations find you. Either way, now is the time to be as receptive as you can to what should be positive influences.

4 THURSDAY   *Moon Age Day 16   Moon Sign Cancer*

am ....

pm ....
You would be wise to avoid jumping to specific conclusions and be certain that you know what you are doing before you embark on anything new. Sometimes Aries people launch themselves into change without a second thought, but for the moment the planetary line-up is saying it would be best to use a little caution.

5 FRIDAY
Moon Age Day 17   Moon Sign Leo

am ....

pm ....
You could find that your powers of attraction are particularly strong at the moment and would be well advised to use what providence has given you to your best advantage. Finances may well respond to your present frame of mind and you should get on particularly well today with people who are also positive by nature.

6 SATURDAY
Moon Age Day 18   Moon Sign Leo

am ....

pm ....
Trends suggest you have tremendous energy to deal with whatever life tends to put in your path. Where others would find some difficulties, you can sally forth regardless. Love can come knocking at your door around this time, and you are able to show a friendly and outgoing attitude in just about every area of life.

7 SUNDAY
Moon Age Day 19   Moon Sign Virgo

am ....

pm ....
Social invitations may well be on the increase, and now that Christmas is becoming something of a memory, you should be in the market for new interactions and for seeking a good time. Someone you might not have seen for ages could well be making a repeat visit to your life, and probably just in time!

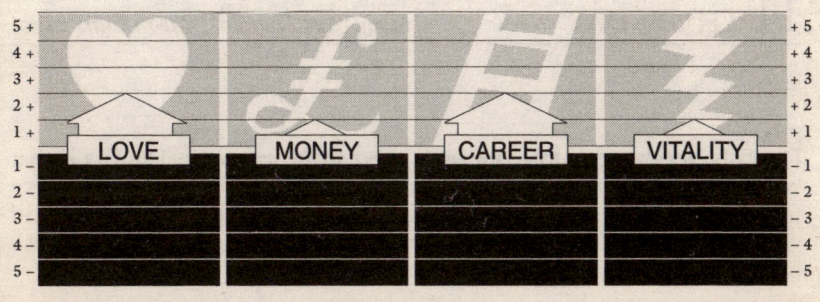

8 MONDAY　　　　　*Moon Age Day 20　Moon Sign Virgo*

am ....

pm ....
A distinctly restless streak is possible at the start of a new working week and you may decide to change anything that looks out of date or past its sell-by date. This is the hallmark of your zodiac sign and you won't take kindly to anyone who suggests you don't have the right to turn the world upside down.

9 TUESDAY　　　　　*Moon Age Day 21　Moon Sign Virgo*

am ....

pm ....
Gains are within your reach professionally, but the same cannot be said to be the case as far as your personal life is concerned. It could feel as though you are treading on eggshells in terms of the way you get on with your relatives or close friends. Being sensitive to their needs and feelings is your best response.

10 WEDNESDAY　　　*Moon Age Day 22　Moon Sign Libra*

am ....

pm ....
The Moon is presently occupying your opposite zodiac sign of Libra. This is known as the lunar low, and is something that happens once each month. You may well be feeling lacklustre, and won't want to be pushing over any buses just for the moment. A time to stick to quiet pastimes and simple pleasures.

11 THURSDAY　　　　*Moon Age Day 23　Moon Sign Libra*

am ....

pm ....
Don't be too hopeful for your own good at the moment. The fact is that you are trying to swim against the astrological tide if you seek to achieve too much around now. Better by far to sit on the riverbank of life and watch the water flow by. By tomorrow you can get yourself right back on top again.

YOUR DAILY GUIDE TO JANUARY 2007

12 FRIDAY

Moon Age Day 24   Moon Sign Scorpio

am ....

pm ....
You have potential to be very quick-witted today and should be able to get one over on people who have tried to score points off you in the past. All the same, don't allow even the tiniest hint of a cruel streak to show. You get on far better at the moment by being as kind as you can to anyone you encounter.

13 SATURDAY

Moon Age Day 25   Moon Sign Scorpio

am ....

pm ....
Getting your message across to others should be very easy at present because your powers of communication are clearly second to none. There's nothing especially strange about this fact, but the present position of Mercury offers you silver-tongued eloquence and an ability to bring everyone round to your point of view.

14 SUNDAY

Moon Age Day 26   Moon Sign Scorpio

am ....

pm ....
Socially speaking this ought to be a time when you can choose to do your own thing. There are signs that you won't take kindly to being forced down any path that doesn't appeal to you, and this is probably not the best time for taking on laborious jobs that you find boring or distasteful. Why not stick to what you know will be stimulating and fascinating?

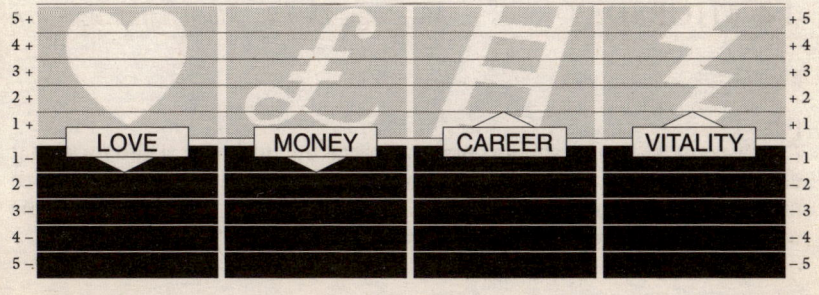

| LOVE | MONEY | CAREER | VITALITY |

15 MONDAY   *Moon Age Day 27   Moon Sign Sagittarius*

am . . . .

pm . . . .
This is probably the best day of the month for getting out and discovering what the world is up to. Your natural curiosity is raised to fever pitch and a few people might even call you nosy! Anything unusual or weird is likely to have a particular fascination for you under present planetary trends.

16 TUESDAY   *Moon Age Day 28   Moon Sign Sagittarius*

am . . . .

pm . . . .
Professional matters can be moved along in an interesting and stimulating way, and you should respond very positively to new happenings and to challenges of just about any sort. Don't be too keen to offer advice to others at a time when you would be better advised to look at areas of your own life first.

17 WEDNESDAY   *Moon Age Day 29   Moon Sign Capricorn*

am . . . .

pm . . . .
If you are increasing the pace of your professional life even more, there may not be much time for social interactions or for sorting out the lives of everyone around you. You shouldn't have to apologise for the fact, because those to whom you are close should understand only too well how your nature works.

18 THURSDAY   *Moon Age Day 0   Moon Sign Capricorn*

am . . . .

pm . . . .
A new sense of optimism and opportunity is around now, a situation that could easily coincide with the chance to meet new people and to encounter situations you find to be distinctly exciting. Give yourself the necessary time to take information on board before reacting today.

YOUR DAILY GUIDE TO JANUARY 2007

19 FRIDAY *Moon Age Day 1   Moon Sign Aquarius*

am ....

pm ....
This has potential to be another very favourable day. The Moon is occupying your solar eleventh house and that enables you to be particularly good in social situations. There are small financial gains to be made, though probably more as a result of your efforts than thanks to any particularly lucky happenings.

20 SATURDAY *Moon Age Day 2   Moon Sign Aquarius*

am ....

pm ....
What you have planned and worked for recently can now be made to pay off. Knowing how to close a deal is very important, no matter what area of life you are looking at. Relationships can be especially rewarding this weekend and single Aries subjects could be looking around for a new romantic contact now.

21 SUNDAY *Moon Age Day 3   Moon Sign Aquarius*

am ....

pm ....
This is a time that is suited to a little reflection, so you may opt for a quiet sort of Sunday and for a day during which you are willing to let life pass you by in some respects. Everyone needs to recharge their batteries from time to time, and today proves to be such a period for you.

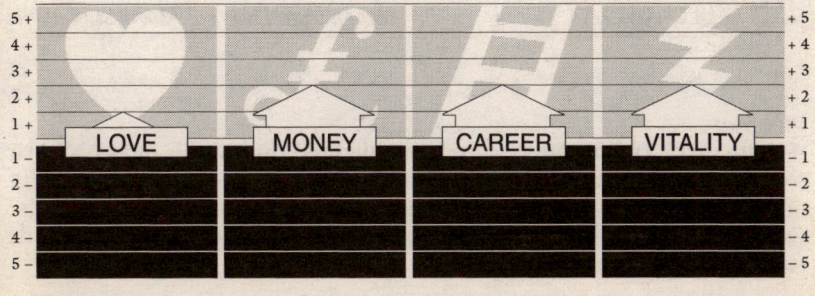

22 MONDAY *Moon Age Day 4   Moon Sign Pisces*

am ....

pm ....
Professional matters bring new opportunities, though there may still be a part of your mind that is centred upon personal issues and relationships in general. It could be that family members have certain worries, and you could be in just the right position and frame of mind to offer a little timely advice.

23 TUESDAY *Moon Age Day 5   Moon Sign Pisces*

am ....

pm ....
Things could be rather quieter than you would wish. This is a response to the present position of the Moon, which is in your solar twelfth house. Don't worry, because things could well change quite significantly by tomorrow. You would be well advised to take any relaxation on offer whilst you can.

24 WEDNESDAY *Moon Age Day 6   Moon Sign Aries*

am ....

pm ....
Now is a time to take everything that life has given you in terms of your nature and abilities and to use them to your advantage. The lunar high is around – that part of the month during which the Moon occupies your own zodiac sign. Levels of good luck are increased and you probably know very well how to proceed.

25 THURSDAY *Moon Age Day 7   Moon Sign Aries*

am ....

pm ....
Group involvements are positively highlighted during this month's lunar high and you are at your very best when you are co-operating with just about anyone. Creature comforts don't seem to matter at all, and there isn't much doubt that you can make the most of a very positive attitude to action and excitement.

YOUR DAILY GUIDE TO JANUARY 2007

26 FRIDAY *Moon Age Day 8   Moon Sign Taurus*

am ....

pm ....
In a social sense you should be in a position to enjoy just about anything that presently comes your way. Although the Moon has now passed away from your own zodiac sign, there are other planetary influences that are almost as positive. A day to remove yourself from situations you find to be either tedious or embarrassing.

27 SATURDAY *Moon Age Day 9   Moon Sign Taurus*

am ....

pm ....
You would be wise to show a great deal of caution today because the planetary line-up is not really working to your advantage. If you have any legal document to sign it would be sensible to read the small print very carefully and even to leave matters until another day. Attitude is very important in romantic contacts.

28 SUNDAY *Moon Age Day 10   Moon Sign Gemini*

am ....

pm ....
Intellectual pursuits seem to appeal to you on this winter Sunday, and if you can't get out and about as much as you would wish you can get things sorted out at home. Relatives and friends could be especially helpful under present trends, and you could do worse than to ask for some advice.

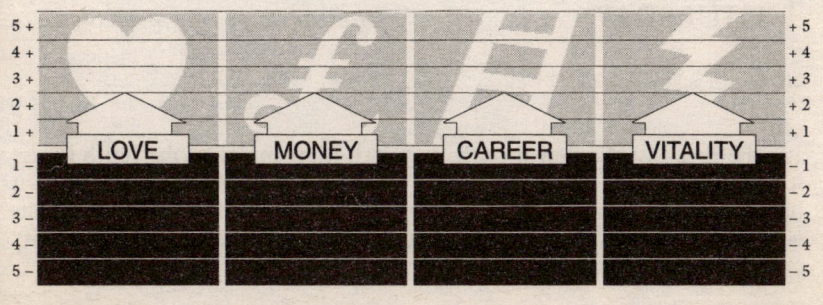

LOVE	MONEY	CAREER	VITALITY

29 MONDAY *Moon Age Day 11   Moon Sign Gemini*

am ....

pm ....
Right now you have scope to enjoy being one of the gang and to show greater social responses than has sometimes been the case so far this month. Routines can be rather boring, so you may decide to ring the changes whenever it proves to be possible. Co-operation is still the key to success.

30 TUESDAY *Moon Age Day 12   Moon Sign Cancer*

am ....

pm ....
Trends indicate a tendency to be slightly moody today, something you should work against as much as possible. Rather than falling out with others it would be better for you to spend some time on your own. There is plenty to do, and a quiet interlude could suit your present frame of mind.

31 WEDNESDAY *Moon Age Day 13   Moon Sign Cancer*

am ....

pm ....
Not all relationships may work out quite the way you had expected, and you would be well advised to think seriously before getting yourself involved in any discussions that could lead to arguments. People who come into your life more or less by chance could have something very special to offer you under present circumstances.

1 THURSDAY *Moon Age Day 14   Moon Sign Leo*

am ....

pm ....
It's the first day of a new month, and with Mars in your solar tenth house it looks as though you have what it takes to get ahead in a big way. You have what it takes to be very energetic and to tackle most situations yourself, rather than allowing others to rule your destiny. Individuality counts for a great deal.

YOUR DAILY GUIDE TO FEBRUARY 2007

2 FRIDAY *Moon Age Day 15   Moon Sign Leo*

am ....

pm ....
Romance and social developments are now well starred and you may well be so busy in a personal sense that you will have little or no time to concentrate on practical or professional matters. You might decide to leave others to do the mundane tasks, whilst you look around for those jobs you find stimulating and even exciting.

3 SATURDAY *Moon Age Day 16   Moon Sign Leo*

am ....

pm ....
Current trends show today to be good from the point of view of having fun. This is likely to be the sort of weekend during which you have the chance to do exactly what takes your fancy. If you still don't want to get on with jobs you find either taxing or tedious, why not find ways to get friends involved in your schemes?

4 SUNDAY *Moon Age Day 17   Moon Sign Virgo*

am ....

pm ....
When it comes to the practical side of life, today's trends assist you to be right on the ball. Anything you tackle at the moment has a good chance of going the way you would wish and this could be considered a green light day by many Aries subjects. A day to get in touch with relatives or friends who are presently far from home.

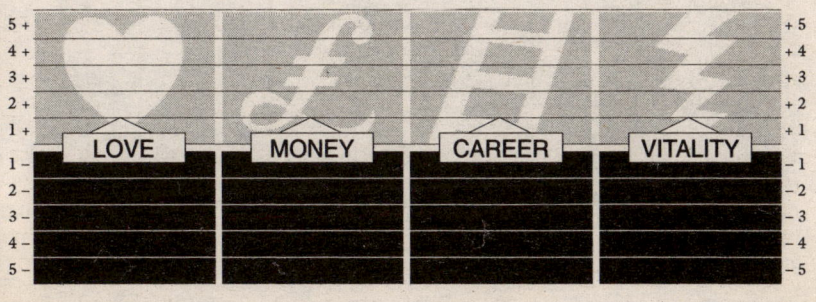

LOVE	MONEY	CAREER	VITALITY

♈ February 2007

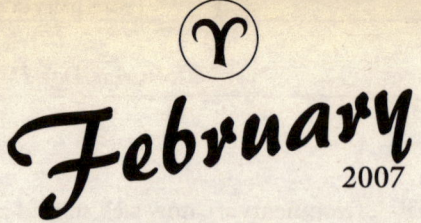

YOUR MONTH AT A GLANCE

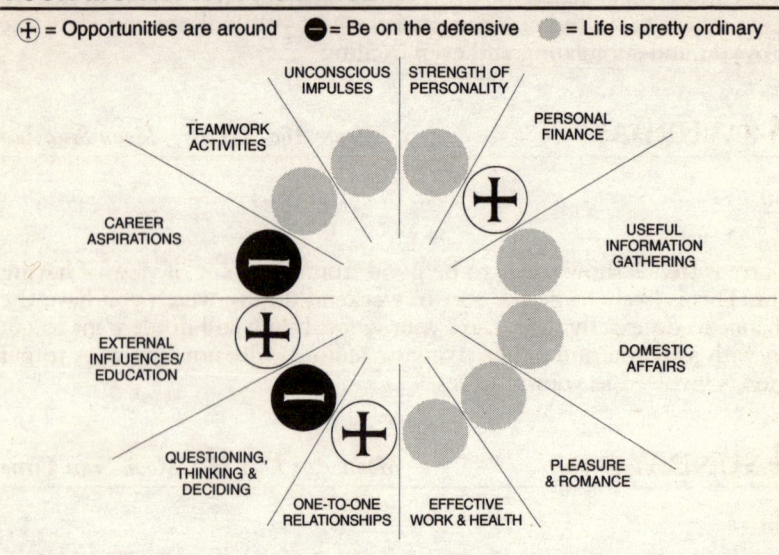

⊕ = Opportunities are around   ⊖ = Be on the defensive   ● = Life is pretty ordinary

- UNCONSCIOUS IMPULSES
- STRENGTH OF PERSONALITY
- TEAMWORK ACTIVITIES
- PERSONAL FINANCE ⊕
- CAREER ASPIRATIONS ⊖
- USEFUL INFORMATION GATHERING
- EXTERNAL INFLUENCES/EDUCATION ⊕
- DOMESTIC AFFAIRS
- QUESTIONING, THINKING & DECIDING ⊖
- ONE-TO-ONE RELATIONSHIPS ⊕
- EFFECTIVE WORK & HEALTH
- PLEASURE & ROMANCE

FEBRUARY HIGHS AND LOWS

Here I show you how the rhythms of the Moon will affect you this month. Like the tide, your energies and abilities will rise and fall with its pattern. When it is above the centre line, go for it, when it is below, you should be resting.

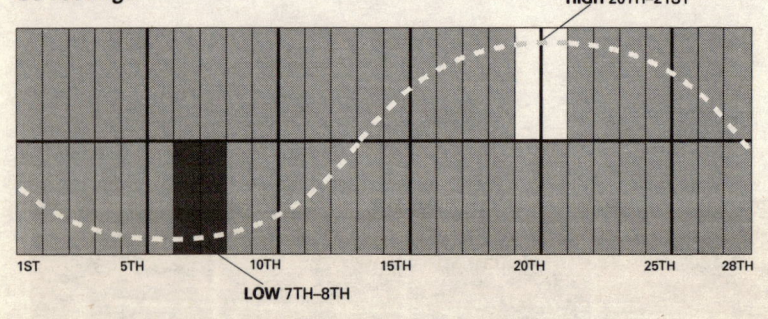

HIGH 20TH–21ST

LOW 7TH–8TH

52

5 MONDAY   *Moon Age Day 18   Moon Sign Virgo*

am ....

pm ....
This may not be the best day of the month for high expectations, either of yourself or those around you. A little patience is called for, but unfortunately the signs are that this is a commodity you don't have a great deal of. Simply go with the flow for a few hours because you can often resolve matters in the end.

6 TUESDAY   *Moon Age Day 19   Moon Sign Virgo*

am ....

pm ....
Don't expect to carry on in the old sweet way. If you want things to turn out the way you wish, this is one of those days during which you might have to put in that extra bit of effort. Now is the time to avoid confrontations with workmates or friends and to look for situations that allow you to get along with just about everyone.

7 WEDNESDAY   *Moon Age Day 20   Moon Sign Libra*

am ....

pm ....
This is the time of the month during which you would be wise to get as much rest as you can. The lunar low tends to sap your strength and might hinder you from making the sort of progress that is common to the Aries life. It won't do you any harm to stand and watch life for a few hours.

8 THURSDAY   *Moon Age Day 21   Moon Sign Libra*

am ....

pm ....
Even if certain efforts look to be more trouble than they are worth, by tomorrow you could feel very differently. That's why it's important not to burn any bridges just for the moment. Simply accept the fact that you can't achieve everything today and allow other people to make some of the running.

9 FRIDAY *Moon Age Day 22 Moon Sign Scorpio*

am ....

pm ....
Though this can be a good day for entrepreneurial issues, you may still decide to rely quite strongly on the assistance that comes from other people. The attitude of your friends could well be rather strange and you might have to understand their state of mind better in order to understand the way they are behaving.

10 SATURDAY *Moon Age Day 23 Moon Sign Scorpio*

am ....

pm ....
Don't be afraid to stick to major commitments and leave unimportant issues for another time. You only have so many hours and you can't rely on the assistance of others quite as much as you might wish. Even if everything you do seems to take a little more effort, don't worry because you have what it takes to get there in the end.

11 SUNDAY *Moon Age Day 24 Moon Sign Scorpio*

am ....

pm ....
Co-operation is now the key to success. Trends assist you to get on very well with groups or organisations of any sort. Be willing to give a little ground in issues that are not exactly dear to your heart. If you do so, you should be able to persuade certain people to lend you a hand.

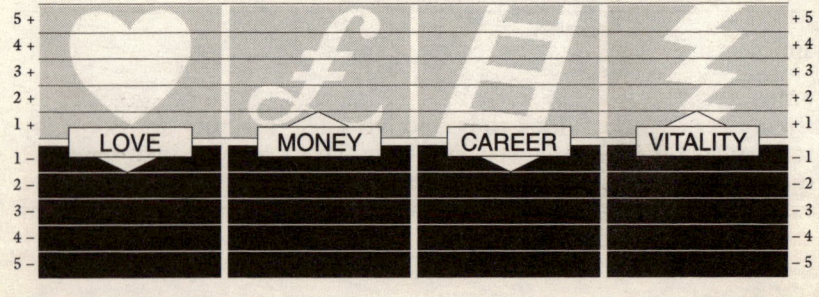

YOUR DAILY GUIDE TO FEBRUARY 2007

12 MONDAY   *Moon Age Day 25   Moon Sign Sagittarius*

am ....
pm ....
Your outlook at this time tends to be very expansive, and present planetary trends encourage you to learn something new. Don't argue for your limitations or you are likely to come across them immediately. It's best for Aries simply to refuse any boundaries and to carry on as if anything is possible.

13 TUESDAY   *Moon Age Day 26   Moon Sign Sagittarius*

am ....
pm ....
Those who are in positions of power may be persuaded to do you some good today, even if you find them somewhat difficult to deal with. Try to meet those around you halfway and show just how sensitive you can be when it really matters. Beware of being too quick to criticise a friend.

14 WEDNESDAY ☿ *Moon Age Day 27   Moon Sign Capricorn*

am ....
pm ....
You are now ready to confidently take the initiative and it looks as though present planetary trends are lining themselves up nicely as far as your professional life is concerned. You might have to work hard at personal attachments, but should find the effort to be more than worthwhile.

15 THURSDAY ☿ *Moon Age Day 28   Moon Sign Capricorn*

am ....
pm ....
This is a pretty good time to socialise, and for a number of different reasons. Not only can you simply enjoy yourself, but there may be people around who can be of tremendous use to you in the longer term. Trends suggest that the attitude of someone on the fringes of your circle takes some understanding and demands patience.

16 FRIDAY ☿ *Moon Age Day 0   Moon Sign Aquarius*

am ....

pm ....
Stand by to make this a very positive day on the social front and to make the most of all the possibilities being brought forward by the present position of the Moon in your solar chart. Confidence follows you ahead of the weekend, and some Aries subjects could be finding new love at or around this time.

17 SATURDAY ☿ *Moon Age Day 1   Moon Sign Aquarius*

am ....

pm ....
There are signs that you are more inclined towards solitary activities today and will be quite pleased with your own company. This is fairly unusual for you but is responsive to the present position of the planet Venus, which occupies your solar twelfth house. If your friends think you might be sulking, be sure to put them in the picture.

18 SUNDAY ☿ *Moon Age Day 2   Moon Sign Pisces*

am ....

pm ....
Things connected to the past can be especially fulfilling at the moment, and you can still afford to be quite contemplative and quiet. This is a state of affairs that will only last a day or two but is really most unusual for gregarious Aries. The Moon joins Venus in your solar twelfth house, and if anything, encourages you to be even quieter.

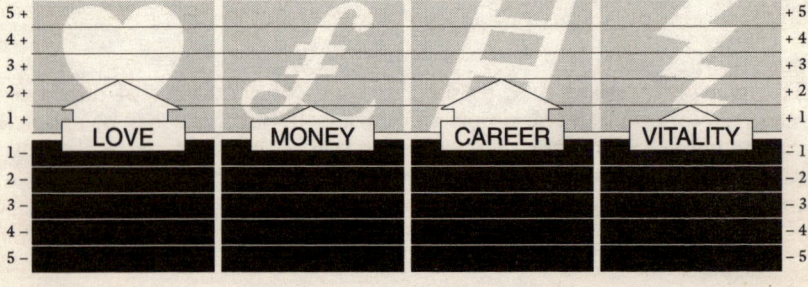

LOVE	MONEY	CAREER	VITALITY

YOUR DAILY GUIDE TO FEBRUARY 2007

19 MONDAY ☿ *Moon Age Day 3   Moon Sign Pisces*

am ....

pm ....
There is a strong pull between your twelfth-house planets and fiery Mars, which is in your solar tenth house. Even if you really do want to get ahead, something seems to be holding you back. Be patient for just a few more hours because by tomorrow you can get everything lined up to move forward.

20 TUESDAY ☿ *Moon Age Day 4   Moon Sign Aries*

am ....

pm ....
The Moon moves into your own zodiac sign and acts like a trigger, releasing a good deal of the pent-up energy that has been simmering below the surface. Now you can be like a rocket that has just been ignited. A day to go for what you think is the best action and don't be held back by people who have a negative view of life.

21 WEDNESDAY ☿ *Moon Age Day 5   Moon Sign Aries*

am ....

pm ....
The lunar high is very helpful when it comes to offering you not only new incentives but also the right sort of energy to push ahead progressively. There are people around who are in an excellent position to give you a leg up and you needn't be afraid right now to approach them in a very positive way.

22 THURSDAY ☿ *Moon Age Day 6   Moon Sign Taurus*

am ....

pm ....
With the Sun in your solar twelfth house for the moment and the Moon moving away from your own sign, you may have to make do with second-best. Don't be too quick to criticise either yourself or those around you. Try to remain positive, though to do so might seem to be quite difficult at the moment.

23 FRIDAY ☿ *Moon Age Day 7   Moon Sign Taurus*

am ....

pm ....
Perhaps you should not overestimate your capabilities just for the moment. Be willing to settle for second-best rather than failing altogether. You would also be sensible to listen to the timely advice of people you consider to be wise in the ways of the world. Giving the wrong impression is easier than you think at present.

24 SATURDAY ☿ *Moon Age Day 8   Moon Sign Gemini*

am ....

pm ....
Be willing to compromise and you can achieve almost anything you want. On the other hand, if you insist on being right all the time you may find you are alienating yourself from the very people who are in the best possible position to help you. Confidence to do the right thing remains strong, though it may lie below the surface.

25 SUNDAY ☿ *Moon Age Day 9   Moon Sign Gemini*

am ....

pm ....
Why not take a little journey and get out of the house today? The weather may not be wonderful but you need a change of scenery and will come back looking at life and specific situations in a very different way. Your natural ingenuity is starting to show, and all you need to exploit it is patience and a quiet mind.

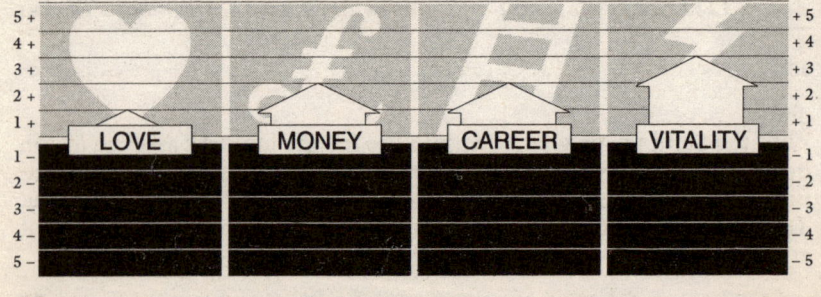

YOUR DAILY GUIDE TO FEBRUARY 2007

26 MONDAY ☿ *Moon Age Day 10   Moon Sign Gemini*

am ....

pm ....
You may benefit from taking a journey inside yourself. The start of this new working week doesn't respond to dynamic actions or to an excitable attitude. Your best approach is to be as quiet as a summer breeze and as attentive as a praying mantis. That way, if opportunities for advancement do come your way, you can be ready to act.

27 TUESDAY ☿ *Moon Age Day 11   Moon Sign Cancer*

am ....

pm ....
Close friends and family members could well have a big part to play in the way you are thinking at the moment. You can get a great deal from paying attention to their needs and from encouraging them to offer you assistance in return. Even if you are still not firing on all cylinders, more positive times are available just around the corner.

28 WEDNESDAY ☿ *Moon Age Day 12   Moon Sign Cancer*

am ....

pm ....
The last day of the month finds you in exactly the right frame of mind to make the most of any opportunity for advancement that comes your way. Little by little you should be more willing to take risks and can get yourself into an excellent position at work. Meanwhile you might also find that love is knocking at your door.

1 THURSDAY ☿ *Moon Age Day 13   Moon Sign Leo*

am ....

pm ....
At last you can put yourself in the limelight again – the place you love to be. Socially speaking you have what it takes to shine like the sun and there won't be many people who can avoid your penetrating and dynamic personality. Professional matters also take a turn for the better – not least of all because you are so progressive.

2007 HOROSCOPE AND ASTRAL DIARY

2 FRIDAY ☿ *Moon Age Day 14   Moon Sign Leo*

am ....

pm ....
With Venus now having moved into your solar first house, this would be an excellent time to look at your romantic life and to make necessary changes in order to feel more settled and comfortable. Few can avoid either your striking personality or your wit. Making friends ought to be a piece of cake at the moment.

3 SATURDAY ☿ *Moon Age Day 15   Moon Sign Virgo*

am ....

pm ....
Trends suggest increased concern for the well-being of those you hold dear. At least part of the weekend can be dedicated to offering timely assistance and the sort of advice for which you are justifiably famous. If you work at the weekend, avoid taking decisions that rightfully belong to others, because you may well annoy them.

4 SUNDAY ☿ *Moon Age Day 16   Moon Sign Virgo*

am ....

pm ....
You have scope to make progress in most areas of your life, even if these don't show very well on a Sunday. Getting out and about is important and you won't do yourself a great deal of good if you stick too close to home. If there are lots of ideas circulating in your head, you need to explore them.

| LOVE | MONEY | CAREER | VITALITY |

March 2007

YOUR MONTH AT A GLANCE

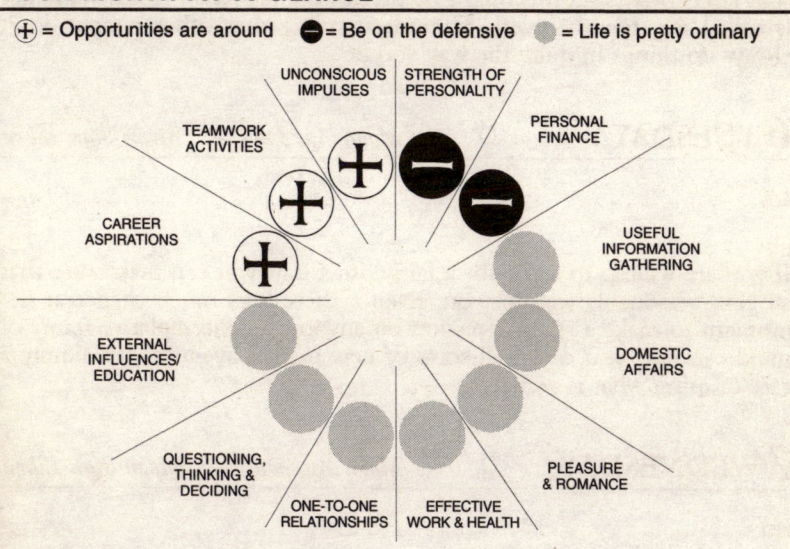

⊕ = Opportunities are around   ⊖ = Be on the defensive   ● = Life is pretty ordinary

- UNCONSCIOUS IMPULSES ⊕
- STRENGTH OF PERSONALITY ⊖
- TEAMWORK ACTIVITIES ⊕
- PERSONAL FINANCE ⊖
- CAREER ASPIRATIONS ⊕
- USEFUL INFORMATION GATHERING
- EXTERNAL INFLUENCES/EDUCATION
- DOMESTIC AFFAIRS
- QUESTIONING, THINKING & DECIDING
- PLEASURE & ROMANCE
- ONE-TO-ONE RELATIONSHIPS
- EFFECTIVE WORK & HEALTH

MARCH HIGHS AND LOWS

Here I show you how the rhythms of the Moon will affect you this month. Like the tide, your energies and abilities will rise and fall with its pattern. When it is above the centre line, go for it, when it is below, you should be resting.

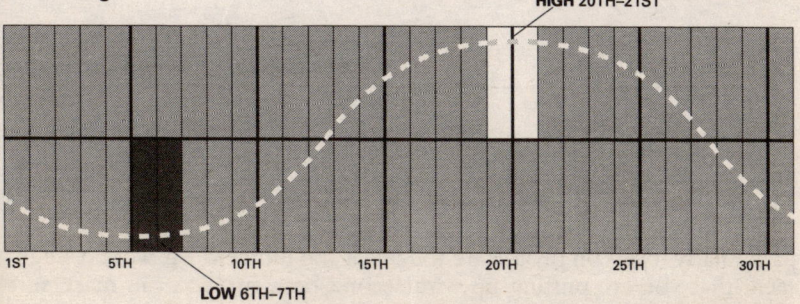

HIGH 20TH–21ST

LOW 6TH–7TH

5 MONDAY ☿ *Moon Age Day 17   Moon Sign Virgo*

am ....

pm ....
There are indications that you could start the day with some personal annoyances hanging around. The Moon moves into your opposite zodiac sign later today, and this might be part of the problem. A little patience is called for, together with an understanding that other people don't always do things in quite the way you do.

6 TUESDAY ☿ *Moon Age Day 18   Moon Sign Libra*

am ....

pm ....
If you are willing to settle for a fairly quiet day, you can make sure that all goes reasonably well for you. Even if there isn't much chance at the moment to make a real impression on anyone, a contemplative frame of mind can lead you down all sorts of new mental avenues. It's simply a case of using what is available.

7 WEDNESDAY ☿ *Moon Age Day 19   Moon Sign Libra*

am ....

pm ....
If it seems as though positive spirits are in short supply, you can help the situation by mixing with people who have a naturally cheerful attitude to life. You can probably call in one or two favours and at the same time you have what it takes to sit quietly and listen to the considerations of some of your friends.

8 THURSDAY ☿ *Moon Age Day 20   Moon Sign Scorpio*

am ....

pm ....
Mars is presently in your solar eleventh house and this can lead to the odd disappointment. Friendships in particular might need extra care, particularly if certain people are touchy at the moment. At work it might seem that you are putting up with second-best, but you can make sure that doesn't last.

YOUR DAILY GUIDE TO MARCH 2007

9 FRIDAY   *Moon Age Day 21   Moon Sign Scorpio*

am ....

pm ....
This would be an excellent period for putting things into perspective as far as your home life is concerned. Why not take time out to talk to relatives and especially to your partner if you have one? Romantically speaking, you have what it takes to be both attentive and considerate – which won't be missed.

10 SATURDAY   *Moon Age Day 22   Moon Sign Scorpio*

am ....

pm ....
Even if it has seemed that there is something of a lull in your fortunes as far as professional and practical matters are concerned, there's nothing to prevent you from being right in the groove in a social sense. The weekend should offer new opportunities to have fun, and there's nothing to stop you grabbing all of these.

11 SUNDAY   *Moon Age Day 23   Moon Sign Sagittarius*

am ....

pm ....
Friendships now tend to be far more interesting than might have been the case in the recent past. In particular, you have potential to be getting on extremely well with certain people who seem to have been rather prickly in the recent past. Give and take are important commodities in your more personal attachments.

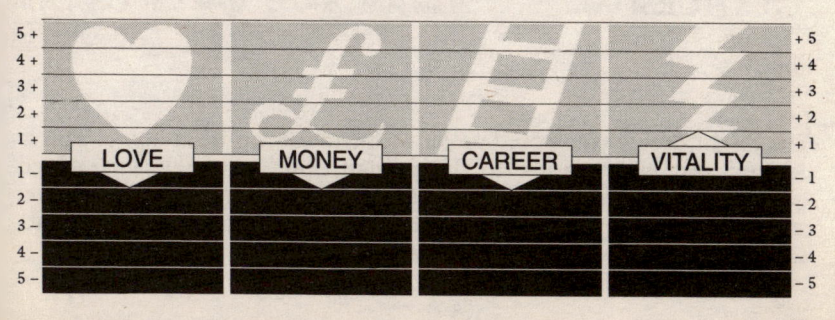

LOVE	MONEY	CAREER	VITALITY

12 MONDAY *Moon Age Day 24   Moon Sign Sagittarius*

am ....

pm ....
Venus is now in your solar first house, a rather positive influence with regard to love and romance. Take your opportunities as they come along and allow the more gregarious quality of your nature to show. Some Aries people could even discover they have admirers they never dreamed about.

13 TUESDAY *Moon Age Day 25   Moon Sign Capricorn*

am ....

pm ....
It's time to focus on matters in the professional sphere, and for the first time in quite a while you have the necessary planetary influences to help you along. A word in the right ear at the appropriate time can work wonders, and you shouldn't have to think too hard in order to make the most appropriate moves.

14 WEDNESDAY *Moon Age Day 26   Moon Sign Capricorn*

am ....

pm ....
Social matters seem to be well accented, and you have the ability to give others a good time. You needn't be put off by one or two people who seem determined to be miserable. What really matters today is your personal frame of mind, which shouldn't be easily dented or altered by negative influences.

15 THURSDAY *Moon Age Day 27   Moon Sign Capricorn*

am ....

pm ....
You might decide you would prefer to spend some time at home. This is a trend that is responsive to the present position of the Sun, which occupies your solar twelfth house. Getting domestic issues sorted now would be sensible, because there are potentially much busier periods ahead and a time when such considerations will take second place.

16 FRIDAY *Moon Age Day 28   Moon Sign Aquarius*

am ....

pm ....
The position of Venus in your solar chart suggests a very affectionate nature for you at present and allows you to show a natural warmth that is sometimes smothered by the more practical issues that predominate in your life. Be willing to tell others how you really feel – especially your partner or close family members.

17 SATURDAY *Moon Age Day 29   Moon Sign Aquarius*

am ....

pm ....
This is a day when you are in a position to reflect on progress you have made of late, so that in a few days you can really start to build on solid foundations. Actually getting anything concrete done may not be easy, but your present frame of mind should be quite mellow, and this is the weekend after all.

18 SUNDAY *Moon Age Day 0   Moon Sign Pisces*

am ....

pm ....
Trends assist you to remain highly sensitive to the thoughts and considerations of others, and this is particularly true in the case of your partner. You could make this Sunday a very positive romantic interlude, and if you have the time to please yourself, why not make a special fuss of someone you care for deeply?

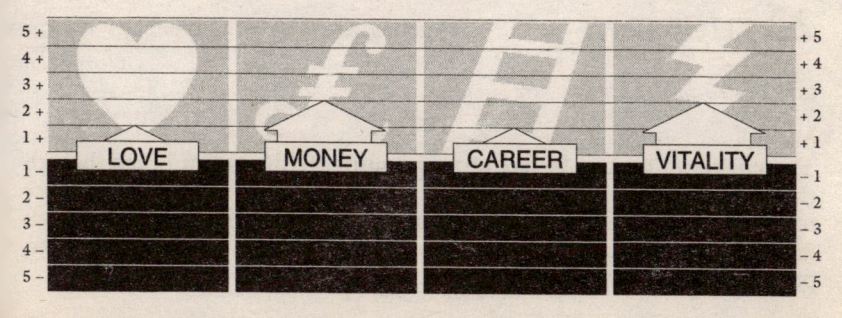

19 MONDAY *Moon Age Day 1   Moon Sign Pisces*

am ....

pm ....
By tomorrow you should be right on the ball, but for the moment you would be wise to remain quiet and simply wait. There are gains to be made from watching and listening, even if you are not yet quite ready to take action. The quiet side of Aries doesn't show itself very often, but it is still an important component of your nature.

20 TUESDAY *Moon Age Day 2   Moon Sign Aries*

am ....

pm ....
Help is available from all sorts of different directions and is especially noteworthy on the work front. With masses of energy on offer and with the lunar high adding extra zest to your life, it's onward and upward. Don't wait to be asked about anything. This is a period during which you can afford to take the initiative.

21 WEDNESDAY *Moon Age Day 3   Moon Sign Aries*

am ....

pm ....
Business issues are now well starred, after a prolonged period during which you may not have been getting very far. If you have a particular notion at the back of your mind, now is the time to speak out and to make certain the world and its dog know exactly what you want – and that you intend to get it!

22 THURSDAY *Moon Age Day 4   Moon Sign Taurus*

am ....

pm ....
There is room for you to feel very optimistic right now, and even though the Moon has now moved out of your zodiac sign, you have what it takes to get ahead. The Sun is now entering your solar first house, where it will stay for the next month or so. As a result you can make sure the more progressive qualities of Aries begin to show.

YOUR DAILY GUIDE TO MARCH 2007

23 FRIDAY
Moon Age Day 5   Moon Sign Taurus

am ....

pm ....
Good news is on offer from a variety of different directions, not least on the family front. You may well be in touch with people who are presently far away, and can gain a great deal by listening carefully to their experiences and opinions. This would be a very good time for some limited financial speculation.

24 SATURDAY
Moon Age Day 6   Moon Sign Gemini

am ....

pm ....
Certain plans at this time might have to be put on hold, probably because of other people rather than on account of anything within your own life or nature. Once again a little patience is called for, a commodity you don't have too much of during the transit of the Sun through your own zodiac sign.

25 SUNDAY
Moon Age Day 7   Moon Sign Gemini

am ....

pm ....
Now is the time to build on recent monetary successes, mainly by watching, waiting and then acting when you know the time to be right. You can rely on your intuition in most situations and shouldn't be fooled by anyone. That doesn't mean to say that some people are as trustworthy as they might appear.

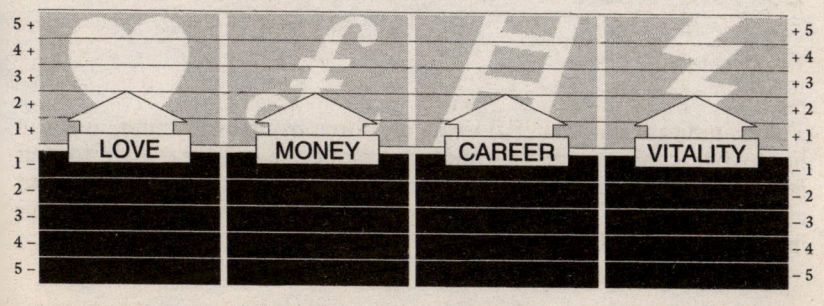

| LOVE | MONEY | CAREER | VITALITY |

26 MONDAY   *Moon Age Day 8   Moon Sign Cancer*

am ....

pm ....
You can be one step ahead of the game in most situations and can rely on both your instincts and your common sense. If your opinions differ from those of your colleagues or friends, it's important to back your own hunches. There are ways and means to avoid falling out with others on the way.

27 TUESDAY   *Moon Age Day 9   Moon Sign Cancer*

am ....

pm ....
Although your powers of communication are highlighted at present, there may be other people around who seem determined to misunderstand what you are saying. Repeat yourself if you have to, but only once. After that it's important to consider whether some individuals are being deliberately stupid.

28 WEDNESDAY   *Moon Age Day 10   Moon Sign Leo*

am ....

pm ....
A boost to your self-confidence is available now and it is brought by the present position of the Moon in your solar chart. You have what it takes to attract praise from the direction of others and can get a great deal from relationships of almost any sort during the present astrological trends.

29 THURSDAY   *Moon Age Day 11   Moon Sign Leo*

am ....

pm ....
Trends indicate that material issues are foremost in your mind, and you have what it takes to make some extra money. Even if you have to wait for a while for it to turn up, you should be pleased that you took that extra bit of effort to get things right. That's why you shouldn't leave important financial decisions to others.

YOUR DAILY GUIDE TO MARCH 2007

30 FRIDAY   *Moon Age Day 12   Moon Sign Leo*

am ....

pm ....
You should be able to take charge of certain work matters and to make sure you are particularly productive at this end of the working week. You can find time later for enjoying yourself and it's possible that a quite dynamic and very interesting sort of weekend begins once the professional worries of the day are over.

31 SATURDAY   *Moon Age Day 13   Moon Sign Virgo*

am ....

pm ....
Whether in business or your social life, you can take advantage of a physical peak. This is a great time for new initiatives of any sort and the only factor that might hold you back a little is that these trends come along at the weekend. A day to make time for enjoying yourself along with your partner and most probably with friends.

1 SUNDAY   *Moon Age Day 14   Moon Sign Virgo*

am ....

pm ....
You seem to be fairly acquisitive right now and might decide to turn at least some of your attention towards getting what you really want. It may also occur to you for perhaps the first time this year that spring is just around the corner, and that could mean getting out of the house and into the countryside.

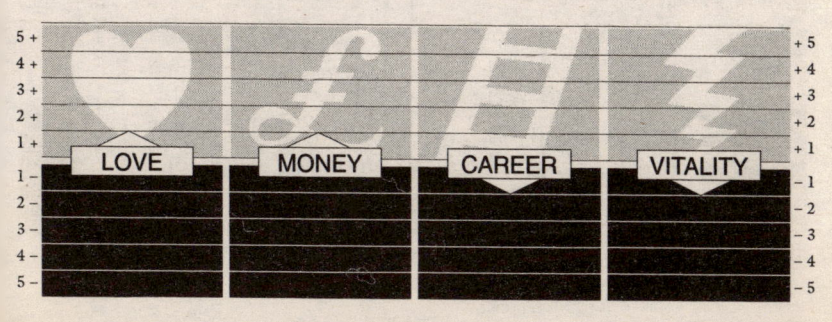

| LOVE | MONEY | CAREER | VITALITY |

April 2007

YOUR MONTH AT A GLANCE

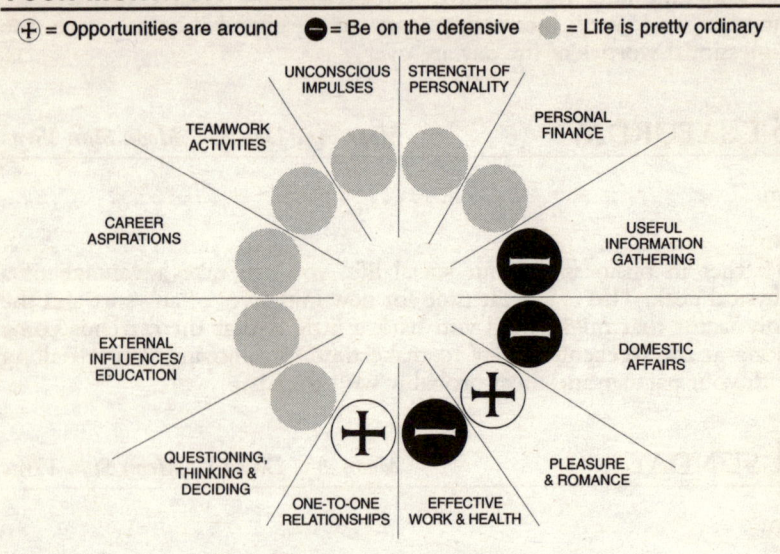

⊕ = Opportunities are around   ⊖ = Be on the defensive   ● = Life is pretty ordinary

- UNCONSCIOUS IMPULSES
- STRENGTH OF PERSONALITY
- TEAMWORK ACTIVITIES
- PERSONAL FINANCE
- CAREER ASPIRATIONS
- USEFUL INFORMATION GATHERING (−)
- EXTERNAL INFLUENCES/EDUCATION
- DOMESTIC AFFAIRS (−)
- QUESTIONING, THINKING & DECIDING
- PLEASURE & ROMANCE (+)
- ONE-TO-ONE RELATIONSHIPS (+)
- EFFECTIVE WORK & HEALTH (−)

APRIL HIGHS AND LOWS

Here I show you how the rhythms of the Moon will affect you this month. Like the tide, your energies and abilities will rise and fall with its pattern. When it is above the centre line, go for it, when it is below, you should be resting.

HIGH 16TH–17TH

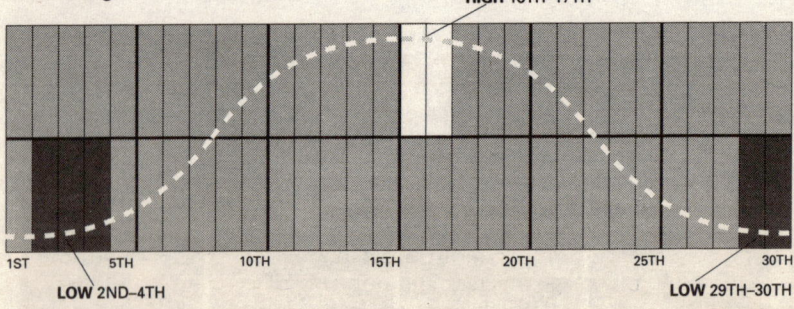

LOW 2ND–4TH   **LOW** 29TH–30TH

YOUR DAILY GUIDE TO APRIL 2007

2 MONDAY   *Moon Age Day 15   Moon Sign Libra*

am ....

pm ....
This is a time when a few challenges may come your way. The lunar low does not help you to get ahead in quite the way you would wish, and as a result you might have to use a little subterfuge in your dealings with the world at large. Just remember that there is more than one way to skin any cat.

3 TUESDAY   *Moon Age Day 16   Moon Sign Libra*

am ....

pm ....
If you are not making the progress you would wish, why not turn to other people for help and advice? This may be something you don't do very often because you usually feel that you are in command of your own destiny. People you have assisted in the past can now be persuaded to lend you a timely hand.

4 WEDNESDAY   *Moon Age Day 17   Moon Sign Libra*

am ....

pm ....
Taking yourself too much for granted amongst workmates and friends might not go down too well. You have a slightly difficult position of the planet Mars to deal with and need to be fairly circumspect in your dealings with others. You would be wise not to leave a job that could easily be got out of the way right now.

5 THURSDAY   *Moon Age Day 18   Moon Sign Scorpio*

am ....

pm ....
There is now a minor but important turning point in the lives of many Aries people. Trends indicate that you need to offload certain responsibilities and to think about them in a new light. You can afford to take time out to achieve this task and not to worry too much if you don't seem to be making too much progress in a practical sense.

6 FRIDAY   *Moon Age Day 19   Moon Sign Scorpio*

am ....

pm ....
Aries tends to be quite extravagant at the moment and you need to be particularly careful, especially with money. Beware of making any unnecessary speculations, and be willing to wait and see before taking any prohibitive sort of action. Romance could well be on the cards for many Aries people this evening.

7 SATURDAY   *Moon Age Day 20   Moon Sign Sagittarius*

am ....

pm ....
This is an excellent time for any heady sort of discussion or debate. You can persuade people to listen carefully to what you have to say and to be quite willing to take your point of view on board. What adds to this positive trend is the fact that your nature can be very electric and inspiring at the moment.

8 SUNDAY   *Moon Age Day 21   Moon Sign Sagittarius*

am ....

pm ....
If you can come up with new and promising ideas, why not put some of them into practice as quickly as possible? This might not be too easy on a Sunday, but if anyone can break through red tape and other difficulties, it's you. Someone you haven't seen for ages could be making a new appearance in your life.

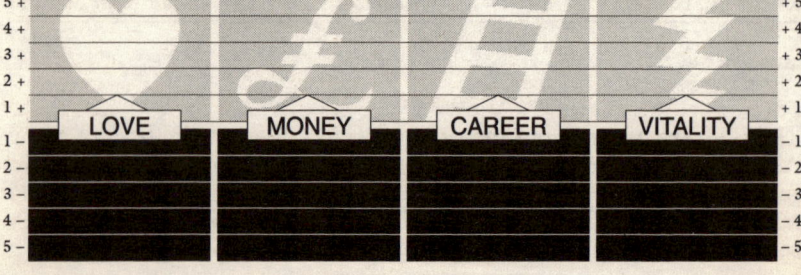

LOVE	MONEY	CAREER	VITALITY

9 MONDAY   *Moon Age Day 22*   *Moon Sign Sagittarius*

am ....

pm ....
You should be able to look forward with some confidence towards professional matters, and can stay right on the ball this week. In a planetary sense there is a great deal going your way. This can encourage greater confidence and an ability to get almost everything right first time.

10 TUESDAY   *Moon Age Day 23*   *Moon Sign Capricorn*

am ....

pm ....
For many Aries subjects what goes best today is your finances. Venus is now in your solar second house, an especially fortunate position for those in business or trying to make money in a day-to-day sense. Looking ahead should be easier now and you have what it takes to avoid making any stupid decisions at this time.

11 WEDNESDAY   *Moon Age Day 24*   *Moon Sign Capricorn*

am ....

pm ....
Although you may not be everyone's cup of tea, you could be especially important to a few specific individuals. The reason you can't get on with the whole world lies partly in the fact that you insist on doing things your own way. Compromise isn't your middle name at the moment, which can cause a problem or two.

12 THURSDAY   *Moon Age Day 25*   *Moon Sign Aquarius*

am ....

pm ....
Trends assist you to feel invigorated and up for some jobs you have been putting on hold for a while now. Avoid getting involved in pointless discussions or even arguments because all this does is to waste valuable time. Once you have made up your mind to a particular course of action, you can afford to stick to your guns.

13 FRIDAY *Moon Age Day 26   Moon Sign Aquarius*

am ....

pm ....
This ought to be another fairly good day for decision making and for coming to terms with necessary changes to your life. Not everyone adapts as easily as you can, and it is important to show a little patience with people who tend to drag their feet. Even if you don't understand them, they do have their own story to tell.

14 SATURDAY *Moon Age Day 27   Moon Sign Pisces*

am ....

pm ....
The Moon has now moved into your solar twelfth house, so things may not go as swimmingly as seems to have been the case for the last few days. A quieter approach is to the fore, and a tendency to weigh up the pros and cons of situations to a greater extent than of late.

15 SUNDAY *Moon Age Day 28   Moon Sign Pisces*

am ....

pm ....
It's important to look after your health around now. Beware of taking unnecessary risks, and stay away from anyone else who is ill. Your system may be just a little depleted at present, which makes this an excellent time to catch a cold. The positive trends of earlier days return much quicker than you might think.

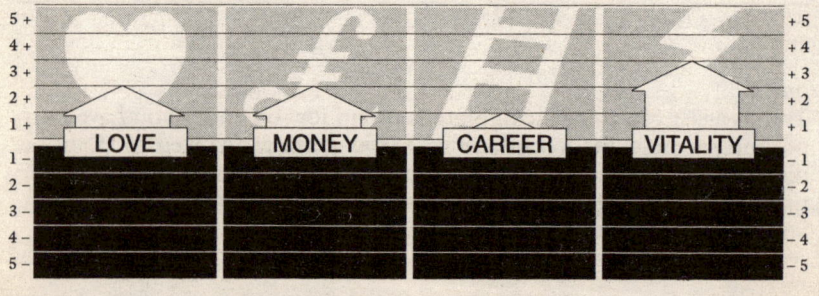

16 MONDAY
Moon Age Day 29   Moon Sign Aries

am ....

pm ....
The Moon returns to your zodiac sign, bringing the lunar high and a whole plethora of new ideas and incentives. Coinciding with the start of a new working week, the Moon can help you in any number of ways. For one thing you are less likely to give in to pressure that others find difficult to cope with.

17 TUESDAY
Moon Age Day 0   Moon Sign Aries

am ....

pm ....
The more you are up against, particularly in a professional sense, the better you are able to feel about yourself and life in general. The time is right to push ahead with all major incentives and not to be too tardy when it comes to showing others the dynamic side of your nature. A greater sense of responsibility can be put on show.

18 WEDNESDAY
Moon Age Day 1   Moon Sign Taurus

am ....

pm ....
You can make use of plenty of confidence when it comes to approaching and communicating with anyone who is in a position to do you some good. There are possible gains in terms of finances and your ability to plan ahead should be second to none around this time.

19 THURSDAY
Moon Age Day 2   Moon Sign Taurus

am ....

pm ....
You might feel somewhat more limited for a few hours today. Mars, your ruling planet, is still in your solar twelfth house, and although it has been overshadowed by more positive influences across the last few days, it could have an influence on you now. Your best response is to take things steadily and certainly try to think before you act.

20 FRIDAY   *Moon Age Day 3   Moon Sign Gemini*

am ....

pm ....
Your personal magnetism is emphasised at present and this is potentially one of the best days of the month when it comes to love and romance. You have what it takes to make a good impression, no matter who you are dealing with, and it is possible that you will discover an admirer you never knew you had.

21 SATURDAY   *Moon Age Day 4   Moon Sign Gemini*

am ....

pm ....
Your strength lies in getting others on your side this weekend and you are facing one of the potentially best social periods so far this year. Why not leave mundane matters and tedious jobs until later and concentrate instead on having a good time? Don't stick around your home too much, but get out and see the world.

22 SUNDAY   *Moon Age Day 5   Moon Sign Cancer*

am ....

pm ....
Material advancement could be a real possibility, even if the fact that this is a Sunday gets in the way somewhat. You can make the most of your natural good luck to make the right decisions necessary in order to get ahead. Today offers scope for you to keep in touch with those who are at a distance or maybe in hospital.

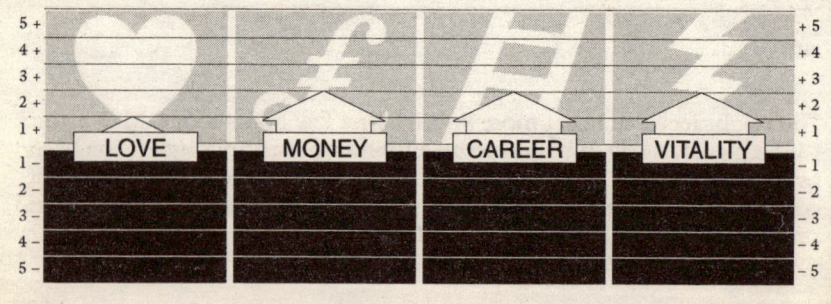

23 MONDAY *Moon Age Day 6   Moon Sign Cancer*

am ....

pm ....
There are signs that loved ones tend to have your best interests at heart at the moment, even if you don't always realise the fact immediately. It would be sensible to listen to what they are trying to tell you and then to react positively to their entreaties. It can't do you any harm at least to bear their advice in mind.

24 TUESDAY *Moon Age Day 7   Moon Sign Leo*

am ....

pm ....
The emphasis at the moment is on leisure and pleasure, which could mean that more practical matters are put on the back burner for a short while. You can't be working flat out all the time and you need to recharge your batteries. Look for something different to do, or follow an initiative that has been put on hold.

25 WEDNESDAY *Moon Age Day 8   Moon Sign Leo*

am ....

pm ....
Whilst this may well be a time for a greater degree of solitude, there ought to be at least one person who appeals to you. Romantically speaking you now have what it takes to express your feelings much more tangibly than might sometimes be the case, and choosing the right loving words should, for once, be quite easy.

26 THURSDAY *Moon Age Day 9   Moon Sign Leo*

am ....

pm ....
Practical developments tend to benefit from present planetary trends and you can make the most of these influences by doing the right thing under almost all circumstances. You have a combination of intuition and practical common sense that you can bring together around now to show you the way forward.

27 FRIDAY *Moon Age Day 10   Moon Sign Virgo*

am ....

pm ....
Trends at the moment encourage a focus on investments and making money in one way or another. This is the very practical side of Aries and represents part of a long-term trend throughout much of this year. You have the ability to look ahead and to plan carefully, and now is the time to put it into practice.

28 SATURDAY *Moon Age Day 11   Moon Sign Virgo*

am ....

pm ....
You can persuade others to keep you both cheerful and diverted during this weekend. Whether or not you actually get anything done in a concrete sense remains to be seen, but there are times when it is important simply to enjoy yourself. People from the past may be coming back into your life now.

29 SUNDAY *Moon Age Day 12   Moon Sign Libra*

am ....

pm ....
The path to progress is not well marked whilst the lunar low is around, which is why you would be wise to take things very steadily today. Forget about becoming rich or trying to run the world single-handed. Your best approach is to respond positively to the overtures of loved ones, and be willing to explore your quiet side.

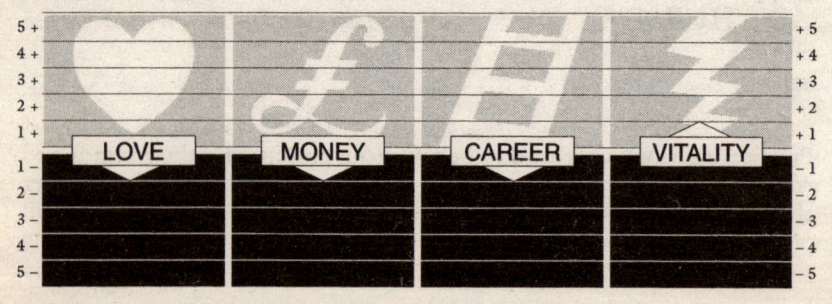

30 MONDAY　　　　　　　　*Moon Age Day 13　Moon Sign Libra*

am ....

pm ....
A slowing of recent trends is a purely temporary matter and so you should not respond to the fact in a negative way. On the contrary, this is a time when you can look ahead and plan carefully. Not everything that happens in your life demands dynamic action on the spur of the moment.

1 TUESDAY　　　　　　　　*Moon Age Day 14　Moon Sign Libra*

am ....

pm ....
It's the start of a new month, and although things may seem quite slow at the beginning of the day, it won't take you long to speed them up again. The time is right to look towards new incentives and in particular towards positive trends on the personal front. You might discover that you are more popular than you think.

2 WEDNESDAY　　　　　　　*Moon Age Day 15　Moon Sign Scorpio*

am ....

pm ....
Back to full speed, you are able to approach most situations in the most positive way imaginable. Taking on several different jobs at the same time should be a piece of cake for you and there aren't many people around who have what it takes to hold you back. Stay away from anyone who is quite negative by nature.

3 THURSDAY　　　　　　　　*Moon Age Day 16　Moon Sign Scorpio*

am ....

pm ....
Mars remains in your solar twelfth house, so there may still be times when you choose to remove yourself from riotous situations and noisy gatherings. There are moments when it is simply important to be on your own and to do whatever takes your personal fancy. You needn't worry if something has to be shelved for a day or two.

4 FRIDAY *Moon Age Day 17   Moon Sign Sagittarius*

am ....

pm ....
You should now channel as much of your energy as possible into new projects that are geared towards financial growth. Don't be too keen to follow the advice of workmates unless you know in your own mind that they are talking sense. You would be wise to remove yourself from any situations that are going to lead to confrontations.

5 SATURDAY *Moon Age Day 18   Moon Sign Sagittarius*

am ....

pm ....
Today is another excellent time during which to start new practical ventures of any kind. Even if there is still a certain quietness at the back of your nature, this merely allows you to think more fully before you act. The combination of skills at your disposal right now is noteworthy.

6 SUNDAY *Moon Age Day 19   Moon Sign Sagittarius*

am ....

pm ....
The Moon enters your solar twelfth house, bringing another positive trend, this one specifically geared towards professional advancement. It's time to get your thinking cap on and to make a few tentative moves that are specifically geared towards making others take notice of both your presence and your ideas.

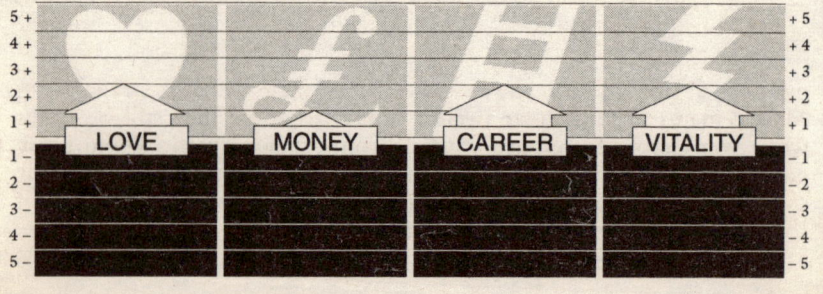

May 2007

YOUR MONTH AT A GLANCE

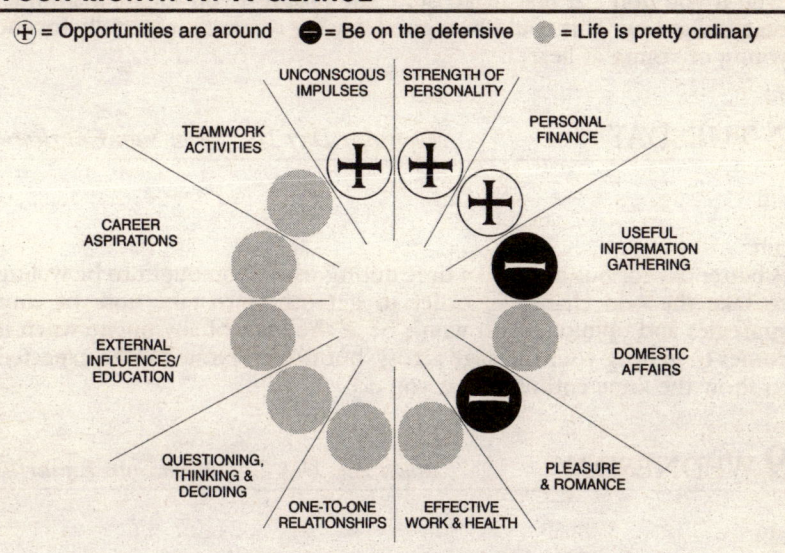

⊕ = Opportunities are around   ⊖ = Be on the defensive   ● = Life is pretty ordinary

- TEAMWORK ACTIVITIES
- UNCONSCIOUS IMPULSES ⊕
- STRENGTH OF PERSONALITY ⊕
- PERSONAL FINANCE ⊕
- CAREER ASPIRATIONS
- USEFUL INFORMATION GATHERING ⊖
- EXTERNAL INFLUENCES/EDUCATION
- DOMESTIC AFFAIRS
- QUESTIONING, THINKING & DECIDING
- PLEASURE & ROMANCE ⊖
- ONE-TO-ONE RELATIONSHIPS
- EFFECTIVE WORK & HEALTH

MAY HIGHS AND LOWS

Here I show you how the rhythms of the Moon will affect you this month. Like the tide, your energies and abilities will rise and fall with its pattern. When it is above the centre line, go for it, when it is below, you should be resting.

HIGH 14TH–15TH

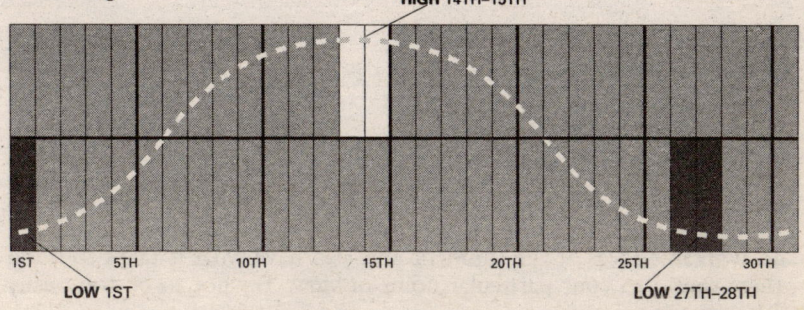

LOW 1ST

LOW 27TH–28TH

7 MONDAY *Moon Age Day 20   Moon Sign Capricorn*

am ....

pm ....
On the social front you can make sure you are very much in demand at the moment. You should find plenty to keep you occupied this week, even if you don't at first make quite the progress you might wish in all practical senses. This could be a good day for romance, especially for the young or young at heart.

8 TUESDAY *Moon Age Day 21   Moon Sign Capricorn*

am ....

pm ....
A better day for business and a time during which you ought to be willing to take the odd chance in order to get others to take note of your strategies and opinions. You won't be at the back of any queue when it comes to getting your message across, but not everyone can be expected to show the same enthusiasm as you do.

9 WEDNESDAY *Moon Age Day 22   Moon Sign Aquarius*

am ....

pm ....
There is likely to be a significant boost to friendships and deeper relationships, thanks in part to the present position of the Moon in your solar chart. You are encouraged to mix freely with newcomers in your life, and stand a good chance of making the most favourable sort of impression when it matters most.

10 THURSDAY *Moon Age Day 23   Moon Sign Aquarius*

am ....

pm ....
You can afford to let your imagination work overtime right now, and this can bring a real boost to your fortunes. The fact is that you have good and workable ideas at the moment and also have what it takes to bring others round to your particular point of view. Try not to be too pushy with nervous types.

11 FRIDAY

Moon Age Day 24   Moon Sign Pisces

am ....

pm ....
Trends indicate a genuine need at the moment for relaxation from pressuring situations, and that means making a conscious decision not to get too involved in certain matters. Why not allow others to take some of the strain whilst you sit back and delegate? This isn't easy for Aries, but it is necessary occasionally.

12 SATURDAY

Moon Age Day 25   Moon Sign Pisces

am ....

pm ....
Current influences assist you to communicate well this weekend and to be especially good at getting your point of view across in an interesting and balanced way. With everything to play for on the social front you should manage to mix business and pleasure in some way, and should be generally satisfied with your progress.

13 SUNDAY

Moon Age Day 26   Moon Sign Pisces

am ....

pm ....
A slightly quieter day is available ahead of the lunar high, which begins tomorrow. It's time to clear the decks for action because there may be no stopping you at the start of the new working week. A day to take a little time out to get to know certain people better – even those you think you understand well enough already.

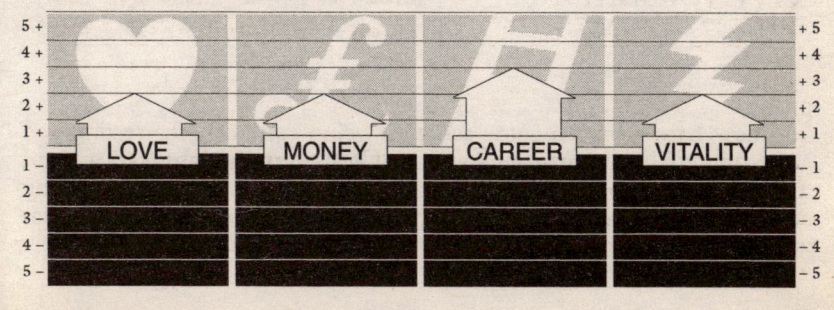

14 MONDAY   *Moon Age Day 27   Moon Sign Aries*

am ....
pm ....
Try to make something big happen today. It doesn't really matter what part of your life is in the spotlight. What's important is to leave everyone around you feeling what a tremendous person you are and how much they would like to follow your lead. Popularity shouldn't be difficult to find.

15 TUESDAY   *Moon Age Day 28   Moon Sign Aries*

am ....
pm ....
Another potentially good day and one that enables you to gain a better understanding of the world at large. It doesn't really matter how busy you may be, you can find time to stop and think and to enjoy the ride. The lunar high can enhance your ability to earn money and to pursue some very good ideas.

16 WEDNESDAY   *Moon Age Day 29   Moon Sign Taurus*

am ....
pm ....
Your ruling planet Mars now occupies your own zodiac sign of Aries and that can only be good when it comes to getting on well in your life generally. Initiatives can be accomplished pretty much as you plan them, and you have all the dynamism necessary both to get things done and to impress almost anyone you come across.

17 THURSDAY   *Moon Age Day 0   Moon Sign Taurus*

am ....
pm ....
You now have scope to come across as being extremely interesting and quite funny. Mercury in your solar third house can increase your wit and make it easy for you to bring people in on your many fascinating conversations. Beware of trying to rush your fences, and remember that you can get what you want with patience and determination.

YOUR DAILY GUIDE TO MAY 2007

18 FRIDAY *Moon Age Day 1   Moon Sign Gemini*

am ....

pm ....
Getting your own way shouldn't be difficult today, and you needn't be afraid of forcing a few issues if those around you seem unwilling to act of their own accord. Working steadily towards your most cherished objectives, you can persuade just about anyone to recognise how organised and capable you are.

19 SATURDAY *Moon Age Day 2   Moon Sign Gemini*

am ....

pm ....
Venus in your solar fourth house represents a steadying influence as far as your home life is concerned. From an emotional point of view you could be more settled than has been the case for quite some time, and you have what it takes to turn even difficult situations into very positive possibilities.

20 SUNDAY *Moon Age Day 3   Moon Sign Cancer*

am ....

pm ....
You are still able to communicate successfully with both colleagues and friends, though it is important also to find a balance in your attachments to family members. There are signs that one or two people to whom you are close could be acting in a somewhat strange manner. Your job for today is to find out why this should be the case.

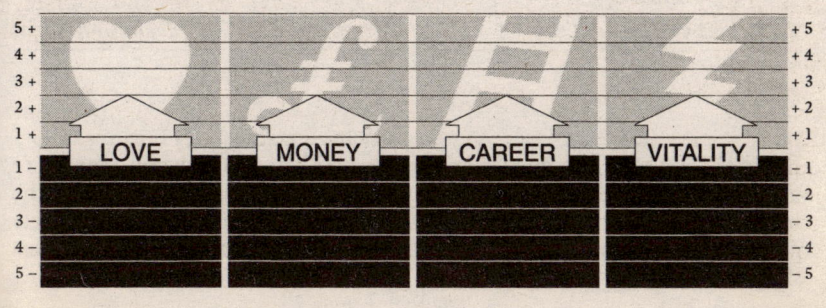

| LOVE | MONEY | CAREER | VITALITY |

21 MONDAY　　　　　　　*Moon Age Day 4　Moon Sign Cancer*

am ....

pm ....
Trends encourage you to seek out the limelight at the moment and you probably won't be happy to hide your light under any bushel. Aries is often a pushy zodiac sign, but this may be especially the case right now. You may have a tendency to act on impulse and to cause yourself one or two little problems as a result.

22 TUESDAY　　　　　　　　*Moon Age Day 5　Moon Sign Leo*

am ....

pm ....
Your own sense of independence is what drives you along noticeably right now, and though this is a very positive thing, it can cause certain problems in your associations with those around you. It's worth taking on board the fact that not everyone's nature works in quite the same way yours does.

23 WEDNESDAY　　　　　　　*Moon Age Day 6　Moon Sign Leo*

am ....

pm ....
This ought to be a distinctly favourable time for having new ideas and putting them into practice. The Sun is now in your solar third house. This helps your inspirational side and is especially important when it comes to seeing how well your messages are received by the world at large. Definitely a day to cultivate new friends.

24 THURSDAY　　　　　　　*Moon Age Day 7　Moon Sign Virgo*

am ....

pm ....
Benefits are there for the taking, both at work and later when you are in the bosom of your family. There is a good balance in your nature at the moment between things that are practical and those that are purely personal in nature. Getting to grips with any wayward family members should be easy now.

YOUR DAILY GUIDE TO MAY 2007

25 FRIDAY *Moon Age Day 8   Moon Sign Virgo*

am ....

pm ....
You may now become aware of a developing though temporary need to spend more time at home. With just a little worry and anxiety creeping in, you might decide that your own domain is the most important place. This is a temporary setback, and in fact need not be a problem at all, if you simply spend more time talking to your loved ones.

26 SATURDAY *Moon Age Day 9   Moon Sign Virgo*

am ....

pm ....
A day to put what seems like crucial decisions on the back burner and realise that everything will come right in its own good time. You won't be able to rush anything once the lunar low arrives tomorrow, and will only cause yourself extra and unnecessary anxiety by trying to push yourself too hard. People might be pleased to lend a hand.

27 SUNDAY *Moon Age Day 10   Moon Sign Libra*

am ....

pm ....
Even if most major plans will have to wait, what is good at the moment is your ability to weigh up the pros and cons of almost any situation. Why not take a back seat for today and enjoy more social interests. One option is to get out of the house and find somewhere really beautiful to go. There you can get to know yourself better.

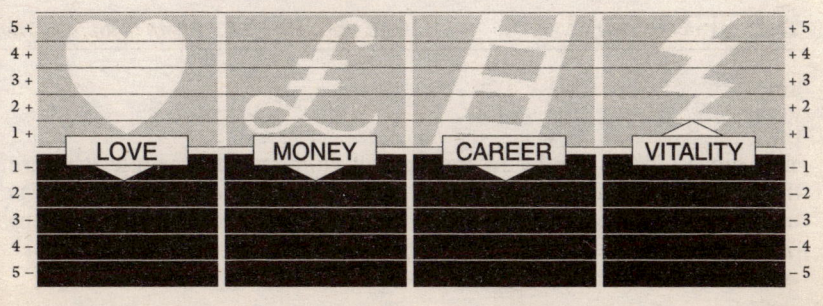

| LOVE | MONEY | CAREER | VITALITY |

28 MONDAY   Moon Age Day 11   Moon Sign Libra

am ....

pm ....
There are now major changes possible as far as your practical life is concerned. Despite any slight worry caused by the continuing lunar low, once it is out of the way the real driving quality of your nature returns. Personal attachments in particular look good and you should be able to find exactly the right words to impress your lover.

29 TUESDAY   Moon Age Day 12   Moon Sign Scorpio

am ....

pm ....
There is now a lot of energy available for dealing with tiring tasks, so much so that you might still be slogging away when others have fallen by the wayside. Accounting for the attitudes and opinions of certain other people may not be so easy, and you might decide you are better off not bothering.

30 WEDNESDAY   Moon Age Day 13   Moon Sign Scorpio

am ....

pm ....
The emphasis at the moment is definitely with home and family, even if this is not a situation that seems to be of your own choosing. The fact is that if people have very definite needs of you at this time, trends encourage you to be on hand to offer all the help and support that proves to be so crucial during this period.

31 THURSDAY   Moon Age Day 14   Moon Sign Scorpio

am ....

pm ....
You can establish good and meaningful contacts with people who are definitely powerful or particularly creative. Their influence on you is marked and their enthusiasm is infectious. Communicating your ideas to others is part of what present trends are about, so get out there and speak your mind!

YOUR DAILY GUIDE TO JUNE 2007

1 FRIDAY   *Moon Age Day 15   Moon Sign Sagittarius*

am ....

pm ....
A very adventurous sort of Aries subject can be put on display at this time, and in a social sense at least the weekend starts here for many of you. A day to look for something very different to do and not to worry if certain other people disapprove. The fact is that you need to follow your own motivations under present planetary trends.

2 SATURDAY   *Moon Age Day 16   Moon Sign Sagittarius*

am ....

pm ....
A new alliance or love interest is there for the taking. Aries people who have been without a personal attachment for some time are now much more likely to find the right sort of individual with whom to share much of what they are. It's really only a matter of keeping your eyes open.

3 SUNDAY   *Moon Age Day 17   Moon Sign Capricorn*

am ....

pm ....
A fairly progressive phase continues and you can make this Sunday your own by taking some notion that has been floating around in your head for a while and making it into a reality. Someone you don't see too often could be appearing in your life again, and might bring a little potential excitement with them.

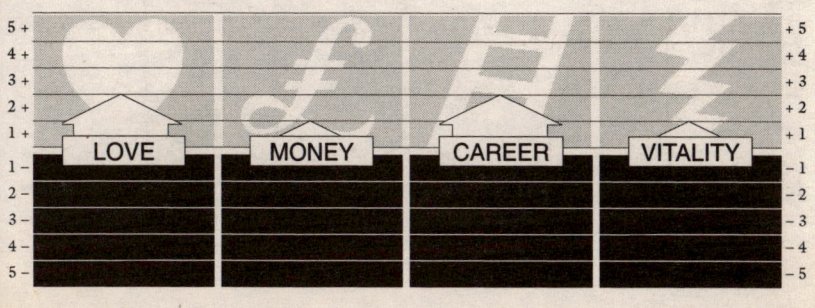

June 2007

YOUR MONTH AT A GLANCE

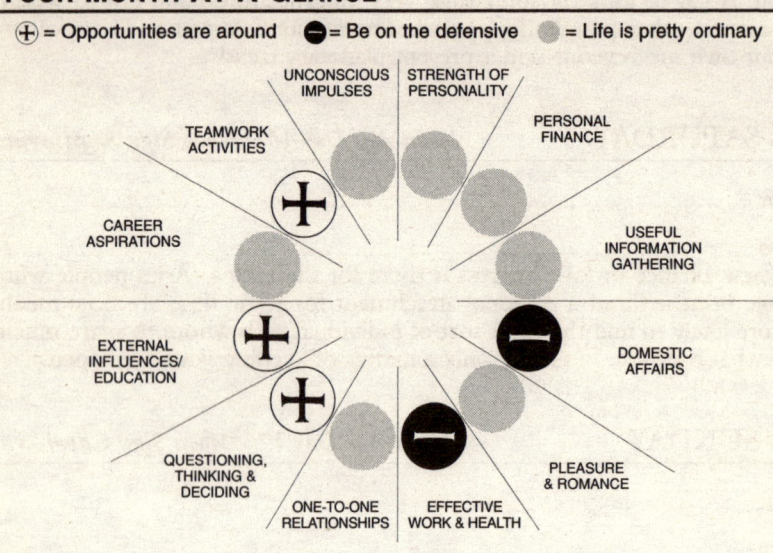

⊕ = Opportunities are around   ⊖ = Be on the defensive   ● = Life is pretty ordinary

- UNCONSCIOUS IMPULSES
- STRENGTH OF PERSONALITY
- TEAMWORK ACTIVITIES ⊕
- PERSONAL FINANCE
- CAREER ASPIRATIONS
- USEFUL INFORMATION GATHERING
- EXTERNAL INFLUENCES/EDUCATION ⊕
- DOMESTIC AFFAIRS ⊖
- QUESTIONING, THINKING & DECIDING ⊕
- PLEASURE & ROMANCE
- ONE-TO-ONE RELATIONSHIPS
- EFFECTIVE WORK & HEALTH ⊖

JUNE HIGHS AND LOWS

Here I show you how the rhythms of the Moon will affect you this month. Like the tide, your energies and abilities will rise and fall with its pattern. When it is above the centre line, go for it, when it is below, you should be resting.

HIGH 10TH–11TH

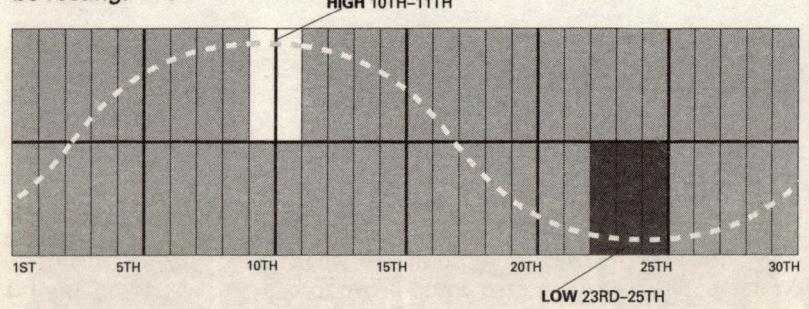

LOW 23RD–25TH

4 MONDAY *Moon Age Day 18   Moon Sign Capricorn*

am ....

pm ....
On the domestic front you can make this a fairly good week. There are some gains to be made at work, but these could be limited in scope, and you might decide you are better off concentrating your efforts where they are going to work best. You can persuade relatives to be especially co-operative – even generally awkward ones.

5 TUESDAY *Moon Age Day 19   Moon Sign Aquarius*

am ....

pm ....
The Moon moves into your solar eleventh house, a position that helps you to achieve an improvement in your social life. There are possible gains to be made in a personal sense too, and you should concentrate your romantic efforts around this part of the week. A time to keep an open mind about changes at work.

6 WEDNESDAY *Moon Age Day 20   Moon Sign Aquarius*

am ....

pm ....
Extended communication is worth a look because there could be some gains to be made through keeping in contact with people who are far away across the world. Considerable effort needs to be put into new plans, particularly if it is becoming obvious that they won't mature without your intervention.

7 THURSDAY *Moon Age Day 21   Moon Sign Aquarius*

am ....

pm ....
There may be less time and inclination to chase social rainbows during this part of the week. A better plan would be to get some practical jobs out of the way and then to get some rest when you are not actually busy. Moments spent on your own could prove to be quite rewarding around this time.

8 FRIDAY　　　　　　　　*Moon Age Day 22　Moon Sign Pisces*

am ....

pm ....
Your charming nature and optimistic outlook can now be displayed for all to see. For the first time this month you can act almost entirely on instinct, and needn't be tardy when it comes to making instant interventions. This is particularly the case in group situations.

9 SATURDAY　　　　　　　*Moon Age Day 23　Moon Sign Pisces*

am ....

pm ....
The lunar high is approaching and it's worth clearing the decks today for a different sort of action from tomorrow on. If there are domestic chores to get out of the way, you can work on them quietly and possibly on your own. There are good contacts possible with others, though they could be just a little muted for the moment.

10 SUNDAY　　　　　　　　*Moon Age Day 24　Moon Sign Aries*

am ....

pm ....
You should have fortune on your side and will be enjoying what the lunar high has to offer you. The only slight fly in the ointment is the fact that your progress may be fairly limited on a Sunday. A day to make the most of offers from friends to get out and enjoy yourself in exciting ways.

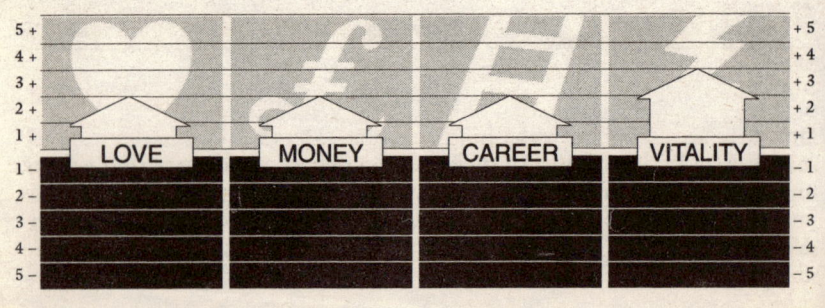

11 MONDAY　　　　*Moon Age Day 25　　Moon Sign Aries*

am ....

pm ....

This is a good time to consolidate your affairs and to put the maximum effort into getting what you want from life in a general sense. At the start of what may be a new working week for many Aries subjects, you can afford to put in that extra bit of energy that can make all the difference.

12 TUESDAY　　　　*Moon Age Day 26　　Moon Sign Taurus*

am ....

pm ....

Meetings that have to do with business are favoured for you around this time. Aries subjects who are involved in education could well discover around now that they are doing rather better than they expected. Beware of leaving details to chance and especially not ones that have a bearing on your social life.

13 WEDNESDAY　　　　*Moon Age Day 27　　Moon Sign Taurus*

am ....

pm ....

Romantic matters and personal attachments are likely to be especially well highlighted at this time. You can thank the present position of Venus, which occupies your solar fifth house. All could be plain sailing for Aries, particularly if you are charming and very considerate in the way you approach others.

14 THURSDAY　　　　*Moon Age Day 28　　Moon Sign Gemini*

am ....

pm ....

Don't be afraid to try something new and unusual around now. Mars remains in your first house and offers a unique and dynamic approach to new situations. Considering the ideas and opinions of others is important because they may have notions that haven't occurred to you, including some that offer some real rewards.

15 FRIDAY *Moon Age Day 0   Moon Sign Gemini*

am ....

pm ....
You can make the most of some good ideas at present, and not all of them are yours. It doesn't really matter where a notion comes from, just as long as you can turn it to your advantage. Give and take are important factors where your love life is concerned, especially by this evening.

16 SATURDAY *Moon Age Day 1   Moon Sign Cancer*

am ....

pm ....
You can attract good support from family members and needn't be easily fazed by anything today. The planetary line-up is particularly positive for you around this time because it fosters a combination of sensitivity and action. It might be said that Aries should be working at its very best under present circumstances.

17 SUNDAY *Moon Age Day 2   Moon Sign Cancer*

am ....

pm ....
Domestic activities may bring you more pleasure than you expected, particularly if others are drawing you into matters that haven't exactly been your province in the past. The level of understanding you are able to show for others goes off the scale and this degree of sensitivity from Aries is likely to raise eyebrows!

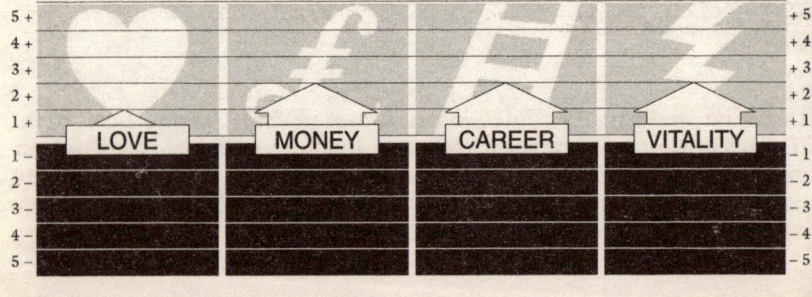

18 MONDAY   *Moon Age Day 3   Moon Sign Leo*

am ....

pm ....
Now is the time to put creative thoughts into words and not to settle for second-best, either from yourself or others. You may have to lay down the law a little, especially if you are in a position of some authority. Keep an open mind about the problems of a friend and don't let that newly discovered sensitivity slip.

19 TUESDAY   *Moon Age Day 4   Moon Sign Leo*

am ....

pm ....
The Moon moves into your solar fifth house, a position from where it can help you to give a definite lift to all forms of leisure and pleasure. Don't be too quick to sort everything out yourself, but do be willing to allow others to take some of the strain. You need a rest, and the potential for getting it right now is good.

20 WEDNESDAY   *Moon Age Day 5   Moon Sign Leo*

am ....

pm ....
A boost to work developments is now possible, even if you have done nothing yourself to bring it about. Today is all about making the most of any opportunity that comes along and is not a time during which you can afford to look any gift horse in the mouth. Bear in mind that a family member could be depending on you.

21 THURSDAY   *Moon Age Day 6   Moon Sign Virgo*

am ....

pm ....
The green light is on when it comes to making general progress in your life and to persuading all sorts of people to lend a hand. Even if not everyone is on your side, you have what it takes right now to ignore those who are openly awkward or in some way resentful.

22 FRIDAY
Moon Age Day 7   Moon Sign Virgo

am ....

pm ....
This is a time during which you need to think about getting on with something simpler. By the end of today the Moon moves into your opposite zodiac sign, bringing a protracted lunar low period. It's important to realise that this need not be a bad time, but simply a period when regeneration is called for.

23 SATURDAY
Moon Age Day 8   Moon Sign Libra

am ....

pm ....
If energy is in short supply, you may simply decide to let others do things for you unless you want your recent progress to slow. You might not be able to achieve much yourself, but you are presently wonderful at watching whilst others toil on. It's only fair, because for most of the time it's probably you who does the majority of the work.

24 SUNDAY
Moon Age Day 9   Moon Sign Libra

am ....

pm ....
There are signs that not everything you wish is going to work out as you might hope, but that's part of the difficulty of the lunar low. If you keep an open mind and realise that anything happening to you now is temporary, in a day or two you will have what it takes to move forward just as progressively as Aries demands.

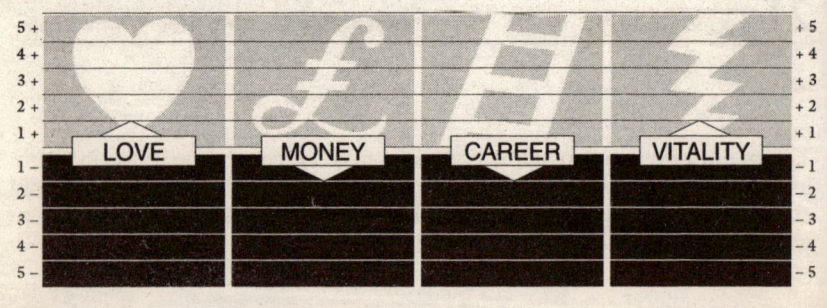

25 MONDAY *Moon Age Day 10   Moon Sign Libra*

am ....

pm ....
This is a good time to concentrate on domestic issues and to sort out one or two little problems that could be cropping up at home. You can encourage relatives to be easy-going and to follow your lead far more willingly than might sometimes be the case. Best of all today, you can afford to feel far more confident.

26 TUESDAY *Moon Age Day 11   Moon Sign Scorpio*

am ....

pm ....
Even if you have a great deal of enthusiasm at present, this might not be quite enough in itself, and you may have to put in that extra amount of physical effort that can make all the difference. A day to get in touch with friends, even those you haven't seen too much of late. Chances are they have something to tell you.

27 WEDNESDAY *Moon Age Day 12   Moon Sign Scorpio*

am ....

pm ....
You may decide to rid yourself of some of life's dead wood at present. What form this will take differs from Aries to Aries, but it could be that you will be looking at work matters in a different way. There is also the potential to make new friends now and to leave behind issues that have nothing to do with you.

28 THURSDAY *Moon Age Day 13   Moon Sign Sagittarius*

am ....

pm ....
This would be a good day to be with family members. You may not feel like doing anything particularly stressful and can definitely gain from simply watching and waiting. It's possible that someone you care about deeply will probably have something to tell you that you will find extremely interesting.

29 FRIDAY   *Moon Age Day 14   Moon Sign Sagittarius*

am ....

pm ....
Along comes a time of the month during which you have scope to widen your interests in some way and a period during which you can get on with a new project that is close to your heart. Meanwhile you might also find yourself in a very romantic frame of mind and will know how to utter those most important words of love.

30 SATURDAY   *Moon Age Day 15   Moon Sign Capricorn*

am ....

pm ....
It is good to begin new relationships under present planetary trends and you shouldn't find it in the least difficult to say whatever is on your mind. Fortunately you can also still be very sensitive at the moment and so you are unlikely to speak out and cause trouble for yourself as can sometimes be the case for Aries people.

1 SUNDAY   ☿ *Moon Age Day 16   Moon Sign Capricorn*

am ....

pm ....
This would be a good time for looking at all sorts of career projects, even though on a Sunday it is possible that you can't do anything about them in a strictly concrete sense. Beware of arguing for your limitations because if you do there is a possibility that things will start to go wrong in unnecessary ways.

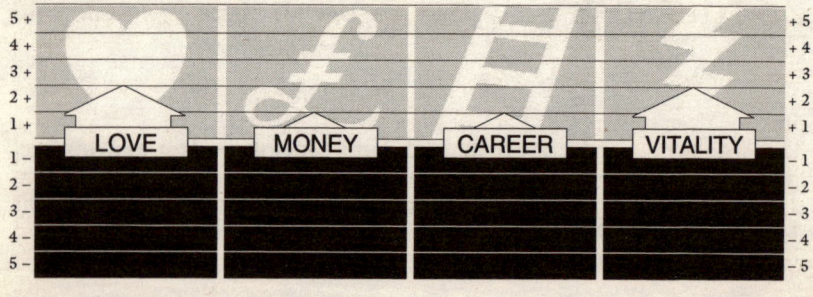

July 2007

YOUR MONTH AT A GLANCE

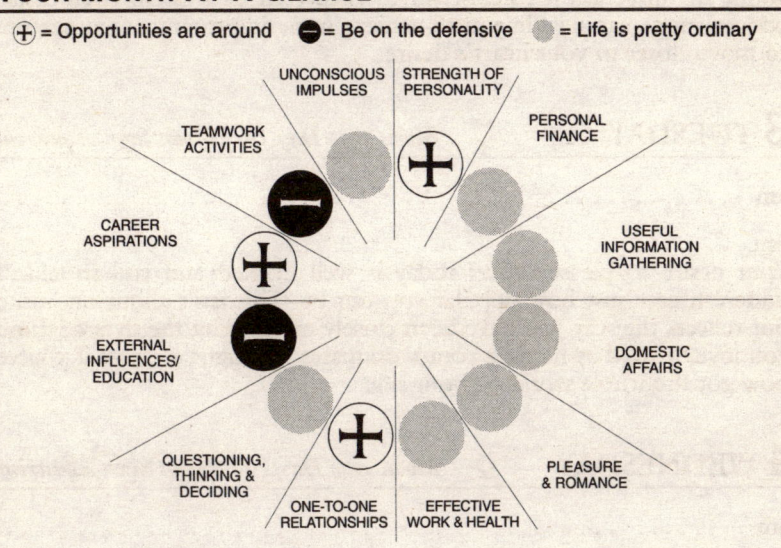

⊕ = Opportunities are around   ⊖ = Be on the defensive   ● = Life is pretty ordinary

- UNCONSCIOUS IMPULSES
- STRENGTH OF PERSONALITY ⊕
- PERSONAL FINANCE
- TEAMWORK ACTIVITIES ⊖
- USEFUL INFORMATION GATHERING
- CAREER ASPIRATIONS ⊕
- DOMESTIC AFFAIRS
- EXTERNAL INFLUENCES/EDUCATION ⊖
- PLEASURE & ROMANCE
- QUESTIONING, THINKING & DECIDING
- ONE-TO-ONE RELATIONSHIPS ⊕
- EFFECTIVE WORK & HEALTH

JULY HIGHS AND LOWS

Here I show you how the rhythms of the Moon will affect you this month. Like the tide, your energies and abilities will rise and fall with its pattern. When it is above the centre line, go for it, when it is below, you should be resting.

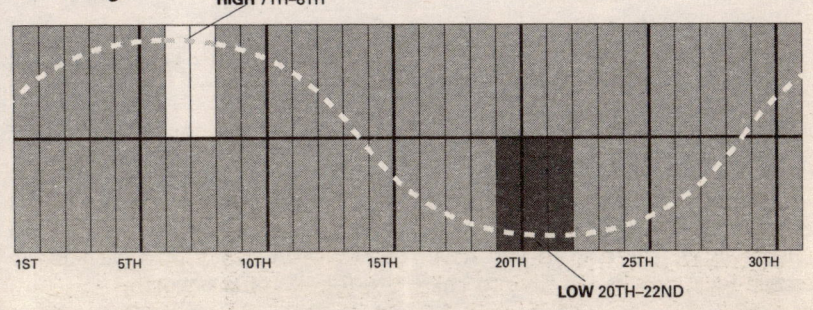

HIGH 7TH–8TH

LOW 20TH–22ND

99

2 MONDAY ☿ *Moon Age Day 17   Moon Sign Capricorn*

am ....

pm ....
Trends indicate that there could be a good deal of support available, and at a time when it matters the most. Since this could be coming from just about any direction it's important to keep your eyes open. Even casual conversations can enable you to achieve some important outcomes and to move closer to your heart's desire.

3 TUESDAY ☿ *Moon Age Day 18   Moon Sign Aquarius*

am ....

pm ....
Your desire to please others today is well marked and you shouldn't underestimate just how popular you can be. This isn't about one issue but reflects the way you have been closely monitoring the lives of those you love, as well as helping your workmates. It might seem as if you've now got the whole world on your side.

4 WEDNESDAY ☿ *Moon Age Day 19   Moon Sign Aquarius*

am ....

pm ....
Hearth and home represent the perfect setting for you at the moment. Although you may feel tied down by professional considerations, you are likely to get the most from domestic issues. Concentrating on loved ones and family matters could help you take your mind away from things you simply cannot resolve.

5 THURSDAY ☿ *Moon Age Day 20   Moon Sign Pisces*

am ....

pm ....
In terms of money matters you could be feeling rather audacious at the moment, and might be much more willing to take a chance than would normally be the case. If you have recently been struck by a particularly good idea, now is the time to chase this for all you are worth.

6 FRIDAY
Moon Age Day 21   Moon Sign Pisces

am ....
pm ....

A happy-go-lucky attitude works best for you around this time and you should not take any aspect of life too seriously. A day to concentrate on issues that are close to your heart and spend time with loved ones. Your partner might have something special to tell you, and it's very important to listen carefully to everything they say.

7 SATURDAY
Moon Age Day 22   Moon Sign Aries

am ....
pm ....

You can make the most of Lady Luck when it comes to choices you are making at the moment. Trends suggest that someone you care about deeply has information that can help you in not just an emotional but a very practical way. It's worth concentrating hard on sorting out the details of a contract or something else you have to sign.

8 SUNDAY
Moon Age Day 23   Moon Sign Aries

am ....
pm ....

The lunar high is the time of the month during which your influence is definitely at its height. Don't be too keen to push ahead on all fronts, because you might be better off picking something that is very important and concentrating specifically on that. Financial matters can be dealt with very successfully around now.

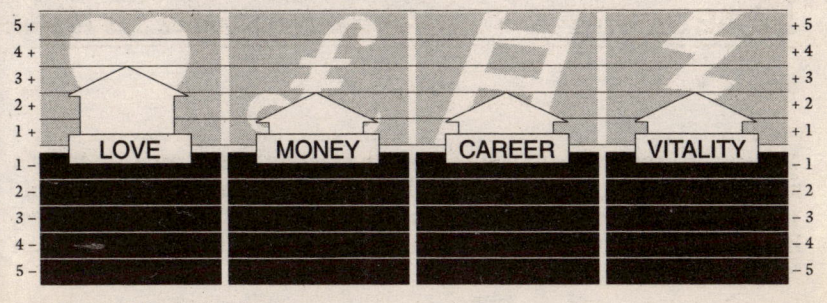

9 MONDAY ☿ *Moon Age Day 24   Moon Sign Taurus*

am ....

pm ....
If family members are in a communicative frame of mind, you may well be on the receiving end. At least it proves that they are thinking about you and that they want you to be involved in their lives. There might not be too much time today for getting on with anything of tremendous importance professionally.

10 TUESDAY ☿ *Moon Age Day 25   Moon Sign Taurus*

am ....

pm ....
On a material level you can now persuade others to be more than considerate and supportive of your needs. There are some gains to be made today, though these are likely to come from rather unexpected directions. Why not keep in touch with colleagues at a distance who might be in a position to help you out in some way?

11 WEDNESDAY *Moon Age Day 26   Moon Sign Gemini*

am ....

pm ....
Trends encourage you to talk through your innermost feelings today and not to be too shy to tell others how you feel. This is particularly true in a romantic sense because it is just possible that someone close has misunderstood your motivations. Financially speaking, you might be able to make this a slightly more fortunate period.

12 THURSDAY *Moon Age Day 27   Moon Sign Gemini*

am ....

pm ....
Now is the time to be enjoying social visits of one sort or another and it's possible that work takes second place to simply having a good time. That's fine, because even Aries people can't be on the go all the time. Routines are somewhat tedious, and you may simply decide to leave them to other people.

YOUR DAILY GUIDE TO JULY 2007

13 FRIDAY   *Moon Age Day 28   Moon Sign Cancer*

am ....

pm ....
An ideal time to put your energies into your home and show real support for family members, especially younger ones. You may not be firing on all cylinders professionally again until after the weekend, and in the meantime you can take this opportunity to spend time on the structure of your more personal life.

14 SATURDAY   *Moon Age Day 29   Moon Sign Cancer*

am ....

pm ....
There is no lack of energy on offer at the moment – the position of your ruling planet Mars in your solar first house will see to that. The only area that might require a little extra caution is money, because you will soon be parted from your cash if you decide to take rather silly risks around this time.

15 SUNDAY   *Moon Age Day 0   Moon Sign Cancer*

am ....

pm ....
Venus now enters your solar sixth house and helps you to have a higher profile generally than might have been the case across the last week or so. You can certainly be popular in a romantic sense and will have what it takes to turn heads. You can afford to spend today having some fun, perhaps in the company of good friends.

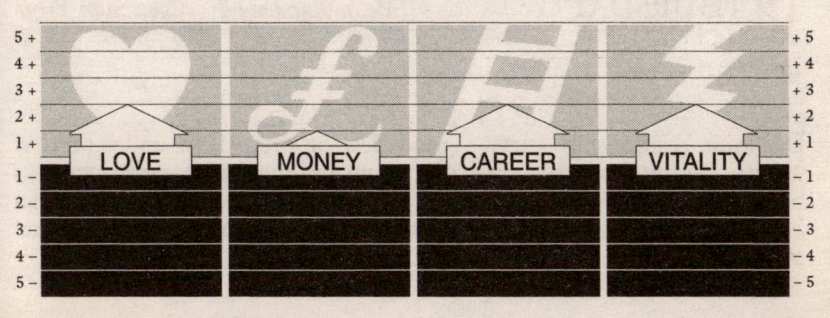

| LOVE | MONEY | CAREER | VITALITY |

16 MONDAY   *Moon Age Day 1   Moon Sign Leo*

am ....

pm ....
This would be a good time to engage in social activities, though it is true that you may be more committed to work matters than seemed to be the case at the beginning of last week. There are some gains to be made that come out of the blue, so it's important to keep paying attention.

17 TUESDAY   *Moon Age Day 2   Moon Sign Leo*

am ....

pm ....
You can now take advantage of an improvement in general circumstances and you could feel that you are now luckier than has been the case in the recent past. A fresh sense of urgency comes along at work or in your studies if you are still in full-time education. It shouldn't be hard now to make a good impression.

18 WEDNESDAY   *Moon Age Day 3   Moon Sign Virgo*

am ....

pm ....
The signs are that your mind is filled with ideas at the moment, and if there is any frustration about at all this comes from not being able to put all of them into operation. Even if people are generally helpful, you may not be at all willing to accept their practical assistance or their advice if you suspect they have some agenda.

19 THURSDAY   *Moon Age Day 4   Moon Sign Virgo*

am ....

pm ....
Domestic relationships carry a good deal of enthusiasm under present influences, and putting a great deal of energy into your home life is no bad thing. But if you are also very busy in other ways, this could lead to a little fatigue, something that even Aries people experience from time to time.

YOUR DAILY GUIDE TO JULY 2007

20 FRIDAY
Moon Age Day 5   Moon Sign Libra

am ....

pm ....
The progressive phase that has been on offer of late may now slacken for a day or two. For this state of affairs you can thank the lunar low. There is little you can do about the situation except to accept that there are times when it is better to look ahead and plan than to actually get on with things.

21 SATURDAY
Moon Age Day 6   Moon Sign Libra

am ....

pm ....
Another lull, and one that leaves you will sufficient time to look at matters in a more thorough manner than has been the case recently. A day to spend time with loved ones and friends, and not to be worried if it seems that someone is beating you to the punch in some way. In a day or two you can get yourself back on course.

22 SUNDAY
Moon Age Day 7   Moon Sign Libra

am ....

pm ....
The Sun is now in your solar fifth house, bringing a month-long period during which you can afford to feel much more content with your general progress. On the other hand, avoid getting bogged down with details right now and instead of getting anxious about anything, deal with it. There is a real mixed bag to deal with right now.

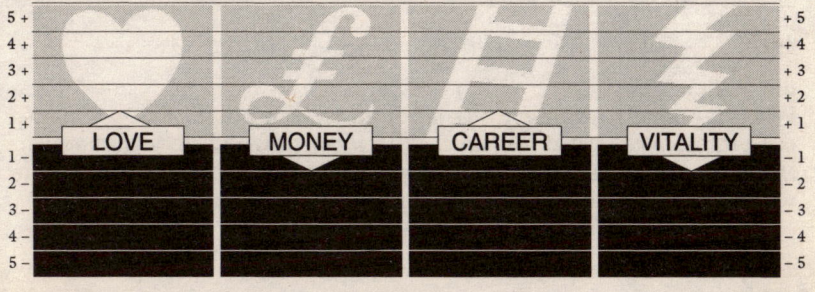

LOVE	MONEY	CAREER	VITALITY

23 MONDAY   *Moon Age Day 8   Moon Sign Scorpio*

am ....

pm ....
There can be some minor good luck on offer now with regard to your career. It probably won't be much, but enough to say you are being noticed and that others do have your best interests at heart. Meanwhile, you have a chance to do rather better in the romantic stakes.

24 TUESDAY   *Moon Age Day 9   Moon Sign Scorpio*

am ....

pm ....
Even if you are restless for a change, this probably isn't the right time for making major alterations to your working life. Better to let things settle first and to watch how things are going on their own. Seeds you planted some time ago are about to germinate, and it would not be sensible to act hastily.

25 WEDNESDAY   *Moon Age Day 10   Moon Sign Sagittarius*

am ....

pm ....
You can make the most of a clear and inquisitive mind at present. Under present trends, discussing matters with others is of prime importance and you can afford to take the time out to explain yourself fully. As far as your personal life is concerned, you are able to get things going better than you expected.

26 THURSDAY   *Moon Age Day 11   Moon Sign Sagittarius*

am ....

pm ....
When it comes to winning others round to your point of view you have everything necessary at this time. With silver-tongued eloquence you are able to make anyone believe anything you want. Of course it would be wise to be sure that you are thinking and speaking sensibly!

YOUR DAILY GUIDE TO JULY 2007

27 FRIDAY *Moon Age Day 12   Moon Sign Sagittarius*

am ....

pm ....
You can turn both personal and professional matters to your own advantage and now find yourself sitting under a number of potentially positive planetary influences. Beware of being too quick to settle for a compromise when in discussion with workmates. Chances are that you can do better, and so you must stick to your guns.

28 SATURDAY *Moon Age Day 13   Moon Sign Capricorn*

am ....

pm ....
The practical world appears to be doing you the odd favour under present planetary trends. You can make this weekend fast, furious and fun. This is the way you like things to be and although you have an astrological mixed bag to deal with at the moment, you can get most trends to work well for you across the next few days.

29 SUNDAY *Moon Age Day 14   Moon Sign Capricorn*

am ....

pm ....
Mars has now moved into your solar second house, a position from which it has a strong influence on your levels of energy. If you constantly want to be on the go, you might not have sufficient time to catch your breath. Make the most of an interesting but busy Sunday, with attention on offer from family members and friends alike.

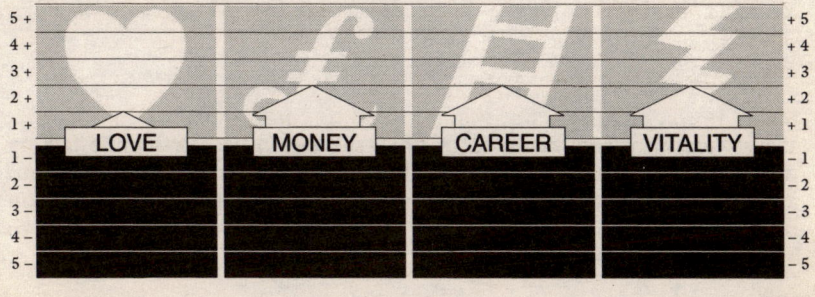

LOVE	MONEY	CAREER	VITALITY

30 MONDAY   *Moon Age Day 15   Moon Sign Aquarius*

am ....

pm ....
Friendships can prove to be most beneficial and rewarding around this time. Trends suggest your popularity and powers of attraction are both off the scale and you need to do whatever you can to make the most of these positive influences. You probably shouldn't sit in a corner and mind your own business because it's time to be noticed.

31 TUESDAY   *Moon Age Day 16   Moon Sign Aquarius*

am ....

pm ....
The last day of July offers you scope to move out in front and to play to the crowd at every possible opportunity. Your ego is certainly strong and you should not hide your light under a bushel. Converting others to your unique point of view should be quite easy, and you might even approach people who have proved intransigent in the past.

1 WEDNESDAY   *Moon Age Day 17   Moon Sign Pisces*

am ....

pm ....
As a new month dawns you might have to look rather carefully at finances. It's possible that you have either been spending rather lavishly or else demands have been coming in from a number of different directions. A day to take time out to think in a professional sense and plan your strategies steadily.

2 THURSDAY   *Moon Age Day 18   Moon Sign Pisces*

am ....

pm ....
If emotional matters begin to overheat, it would be worthwhile talking things through with your partner. This is no time to lose your temper and it's very important to show how sensitive you are capable of being. You may feel wronged over a particular situation but you would be wise to avoid gloating about the fact.

YOUR DAILY GUIDE TO AUGUST 2007

3 FRIDAY
Moon Age Day 19   Moon Sign Aries

am ....

pm ....
Right now you can make the very most of both personal and professional aims. Almost anything you have in your mind can be attained whilst the lunar high is around and you can also achieve a high degree of popularity with some important people. Strike whilst the iron is hot in terms of professional matters.

4 SATURDAY
Moon Age Day 20   Moon Sign Aries

am ....

pm ....
Energies remain in the ascendant and you shouldn't find it hard to get your own way when it matters the most. Even if not everyone performs quite the way you would have expected, you have sufficient energy to do both your job and theirs if necessary. It's worth showing strong support for all family members and close friends.

5 SUNDAY
Moon Age Day 21   Moon Sign Taurus

am ....

pm ....
Looking hard at financial aspects of your life you might discover that this is the time to put on the brakes where specific expenditure is concerned. It may be better to lose out a little in the short term rather than to find matters even more difficult later. Pointless speculation of any sort should probably be avoided for the moment.

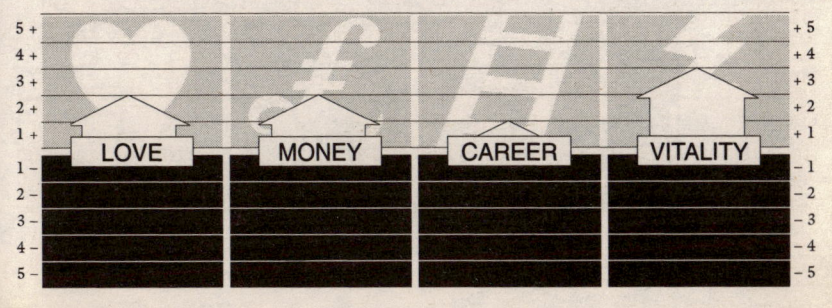

| LOVE | MONEY | CAREER | VITALITY |

August 2007

YOUR MONTH AT A GLANCE

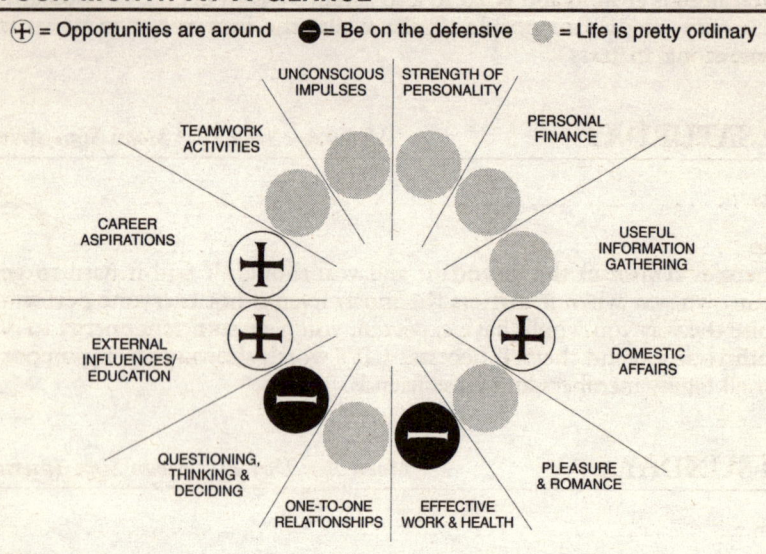

⊕ = Opportunities are around   ⊖ = Be on the defensive   ● = Life is pretty ordinary

- UNCONSCIOUS IMPULSES
- STRENGTH OF PERSONALITY
- TEAMWORK ACTIVITIES
- PERSONAL FINANCE
- CAREER ASPIRATIONS ⊕
- USEFUL INFORMATION GATHERING
- EXTERNAL INFLUENCES/EDUCATION ⊕
- DOMESTIC AFFAIRS ⊕
- QUESTIONING, THINKING & DECIDING
- ONE-TO-ONE RELATIONSHIPS ⊖
- EFFECTIVE WORK & HEALTH ⊖
- PLEASURE & ROMANCE

AUGUST HIGHS AND LOWS

Here I show you how the rhythms of the Moon will affect you this month. Like the tide, your energies and abilities will rise and fall with its pattern. When it is above the centre line, go for it, when it is below, you should be resting.

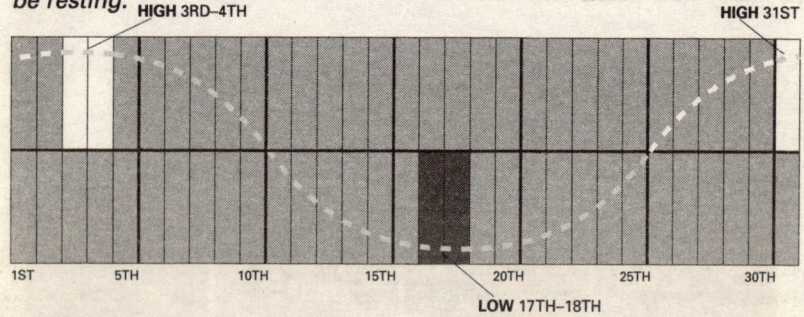

HIGH 3RD–4TH

HIGH 31ST

LOW 17TH–18TH

6 MONDAY *Moon Age Day 22   Moon Sign Taurus*

am ....

pm ....
Looking at hard financial facts is part of what today is about, and you would be well advised not to take any unnecessary monetary risks just for the moment. Be careful to check figures and take some advice if necessary. People from the past could well come back into your life under present influences.

7 TUESDAY *Moon Age Day 23   Moon Sign Taurus*

am ....

pm ....
If you find yourself involved in any discussions today, it's important that these are not allowed to turn into arguments. Aries is potentially quite confrontational at present and you might need to count to ten on occasions. Romance looks fairly settled, and your partner is someone with whom you shouldn't fall out.

8 WEDNESDAY *Moon Age Day 24   Moon Sign Gemini*

am ....

pm ....
A day to avoid making snap decisions and to think about situations very carefully before you commit yourself. Normally Aries thinks on the hoof, but this is not advisable under present trends. You can afford to keep an open mind about a friend or family member who seems to be behaving in a less than typical way.

9 THURSDAY *Moon Age Day 25   Moon Sign Gemini*

am ....

pm ....
Whatever is happening domestically should encourage you to feel contented with life and there are gains to be made at home. The situation regarding work is less certain, and there is just a slight possibility that you will fall out with the very people who are in the best possible position to lend you a hand.

10 FRIDAY *Moon Age Day 26   Moon Sign Cancer*

am ....

pm ....
Venus is in your solar fifth house and in just the right position to help you achieve a greater level of popularity. This is a wave you can successfully ride if you are sensible and if you avoid getting grumpy about things that aren't really worth the effort. Getting it just right is not very easy for Aries at present.

11 SATURDAY *Moon Age Day 27   Moon Sign Cancer*

am ....

pm ....
Trends encourage you to be open to new social experiences and to spend at least part of Saturday doing something that isn't really important but is deeply enjoyable. Creative potential appears to be very good and there is the chance that you will come up with an idea that turns out to be more than just a hunch.

12 SUNDAY *Moon Age Day 28   Moon Sign Leo*

am ....

pm ....
You are now entering a period during which it is good to be yourself, and you should not allow any sort of affectation to creep in. Trying to be something you are not is a waste of time and in any case others like you the way you are. Blunt and a little outspoken you might be, but your honesty shines out.

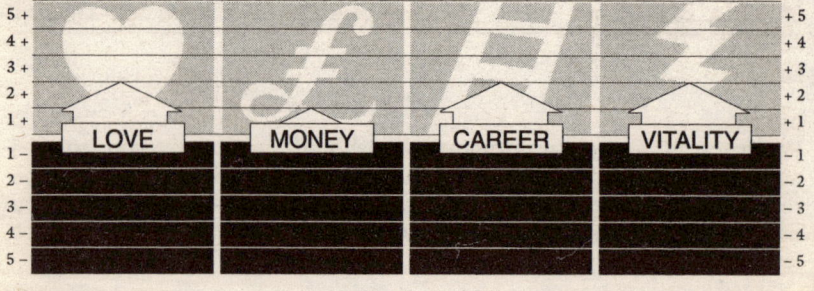

YOUR DAILY GUIDE TO AUGUST 2007

13 MONDAY *Moon Age Day 0   Moon Sign Leo*

am ....

pm ....
You are now entering a potentially high-energy period when you can definitely put the true nature of Aries on display. Even if you are acting on impulse there is every possibility that you will get things right first time and that you have what it takes to bring a touch of excitement into your own life and that of others.

14 TUESDAY *Moon Age Day 1   Moon Sign Virgo*

am ....

pm ....
You have potential to be even more talkative than usual at the moment, and many of the people you come across might think you have swallowed a dictionary. Getting your message across is important, and this is especially the case at work. You needn't hold back, because the planets are on your side when it comes to getting on.

15 WEDNESDAY *Moon Age Day 2   Moon Sign Virgo*

am ....

pm ....
Concentrate on being efficient by all means, especially at work, but when the daily toil is out of the way you can afford to find ways to relax. You can't keep up the sort of pressure you are placing yourself under twenty-four hours a day, and you need some sort of diversion. Friends could show you the way forward if you listen to them.

16 THURSDAY *Moon Age Day 3   Moon Sign Virgo*

am ....

pm ....
Making progress may not be very easy for the next few days. By this afternoon you will be under the influence of the lunar low and might well discover that life is throwing a few obstacles in your path. If you can laugh at these, or at the very least take them in your stride, you can still find yourself making some headway.

17 FRIDAY *Moon Age Day 4   Moon Sign Libra*

am ....

pm ....
Your mind tends to turn inwards around this time, and this is a normal response when the lunar low is about. This doesn't mean being out of sorts or depressed, but it is a contemplative period and one during which a great deal can be achieved – though in an internal sense. A day to keep a sense of proportion in any sporting activities.

18 SATURDAY *Moon Age Day 5   Moon Sign Libra*

am ....

pm ....
There are signs that you might have trouble adapting to certain situations, and this could come as something of a shock to a person who is usually able to modify their stance in a moment. Once again you can blame the position of the Moon, but you should be able to change matters for the better by the end of the afternoon.

19 SUNDAY *Moon Age Day 6   Moon Sign Scorpio*

am ....

pm ....
In terms of progress you can make quite a difference to life by simply putting in that extra bit of effort that seemed impossible across the last few days. The time is right to review your recent decisions, particularly those of a financial nature. It could be that your judgement was clouded and that you were not seeing things properly.

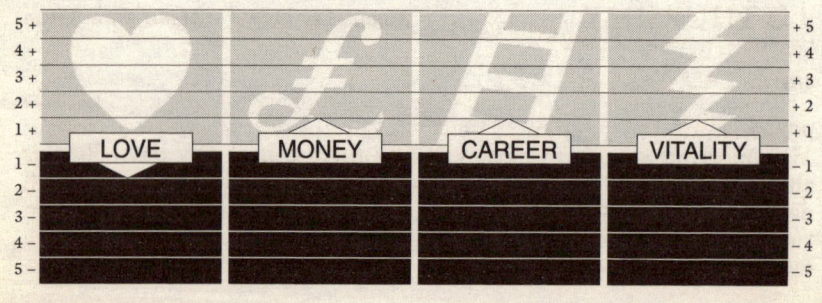

YOUR DAILY GUIDE TO AUGUST 2007

20 MONDAY *Moon Age Day 7   Moon Sign Scorpio*

am ....

pm ....
This might feel like a missing day in some ways because no matter what you do, it seems as though it makes very little difference. This is a temporary hiccup and one best dealt with by way of humour. It's possible that someone you know well could have some important news for you by the end of the day.

21 TUESDAY *Moon Age Day 8   Moon Sign Scorpio*

am ....

pm ....
There is information about that you can turn to your advantage around this time. Simply keep your ears open and don't be afraid to indulge in a little gossip. Aries is not usually one for small talk, but there are times when you need to know who is saying what about who – and why.

22 WEDNESDAY *Moon Age Day 9   Moon Sign Sagittarius*

am ....

pm ....
There is a now a favourable emphasis on love and relationships generally. Finding the right words to say 'I love you' shouldn't be at all difficult, and no trace of embarrassment is likely to creep in. You need the support that comes from personal attachments and this should be readily available.

23 THURSDAY *Moon Age Day 10   Moon Sign Sagittarius*

am ....

pm ....
It looks as though it would be better to simply allow matters to follow their natural course as far as your work is concerned, which leaves you with more time to do whatever takes your fancy. One option would be to get out and about, enjoying the summer weather and maybe even opting for a hastily planned journey.

24 FRIDAY *Moon Age Day 11   Moon Sign Capricorn*

am . . . .

pm . . . .
There may be changes to deal with that you didn't expect, and this fact alone can be annoying, especially when it is realised how much effort Aries puts into planning things of a practical nature. Your best approach is simply to go with the flow for once, because you also have the ability to act impulsively when it matters the most.

25 SATURDAY *Moon Age Day 12   Moon Sign Capricorn*

am . . . .

pm . . . .
You can afford to put professional and career tactics on hold for the weekend. Be quite specific about your desire to enjoy yourself and let those around you know that you are up for a good time. For a day or two it would be best to let others make some of the decisions, whilst you simply enjoy the results.

26 SUNDAY *Moon Age Day 13   Moon Sign Aquarius*

am . . . .

pm . . . .
Events may now conspire in such a way that you find it difficult to respond to them positively. Giving what you are to relationships should be less of a problem and this is a Sunday during which you can be warm and considerate, and a time when it is possible to find things to do that enchant almost everyone.

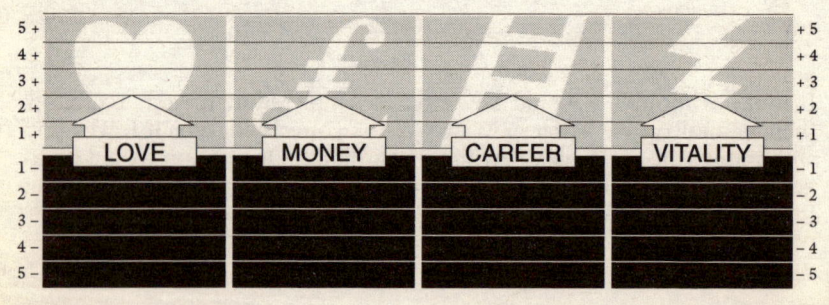

27 MONDAY *Moon Age Day 14   Moon Sign Aquarius*

am . . . .

pm . . . .
Even if your mind is working sharply, there may still be times when the decisions you make seem to have been the wrong ones. It's important to stick to your guns because you will usually prove to have been right in the end. Support is available from friends, though they may make certain demands of you today.

28 TUESDAY *Moon Age Day 15   Moon Sign Aquarius*

am . . . .

pm . . . .
A few personal setbacks are possible, and you need to be sure that you are on the ball when it comes to decisions that have a bearing on your life for some time to come. It might be worth talking to someone you know to be wise and listening carefully to what they have to say. Even an Aries subject can't know everything!

29 WEDNESDAY *Moon Age Day 16   Moon Sign Pisces*

am . . . .

pm . . . .
Trends now assist you to be shrewd and practical – just right for getting on side with situations that have others reeling. You can persuade people who have an influence on your life to pay attention at the moment and so this is an ideal time to shine. Giving the best of what you are suddenly becomes easy.

30 THURSDAY *Moon Age Day 17   Moon Sign Pisces*

am . . . .

pm . . . .
In just a few hours the lunar high comes along, but in the meantime you would be wise to be just a little circumspect. There is a tendency for you to vacillate early in the day but as the hours advance you can become more and more certain of your point of view. By the evening you can make it clear you are in the market for a good time.

31 FRIDAY
Moon Age Day 18   Moon Sign Aries

am ....
pm ....
One of the best days for some time is possible if you are willing to take any bull by the horns. Don't allow others to challenge your authority and make certain everyone knows your opinion. This ought to be an ideal day for making money, even if some of it comes from unexpected directions.

1 SATURDAY
Moon Age Day 19   Moon Sign Aries

am ....
pm ....
You can gain from taking the initiative in almost any situation, and need to be quite certain of your point of view. The weekend offers new opportunities, particularly for having fun. You can definitely put the sporting side of Aries on display and you shouldn't need much encouragement to go for gold.

2 SUNDAY
Moon Age Day 20   Moon Sign Taurus

am ....
pm ....
You can come across good opportunities for getting ahead, but there might also be a few frustrations around at this time. Rely on the help that others are willing to offer and don't try to achieve everything for yourself. There are some unusual circumstances associated with your personal life.

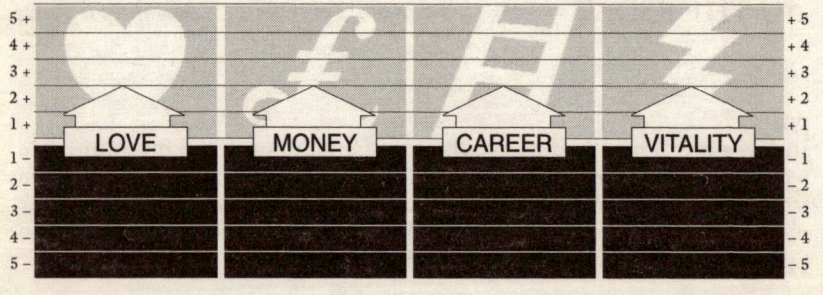

September 2007

YOUR MONTH AT A GLANCE

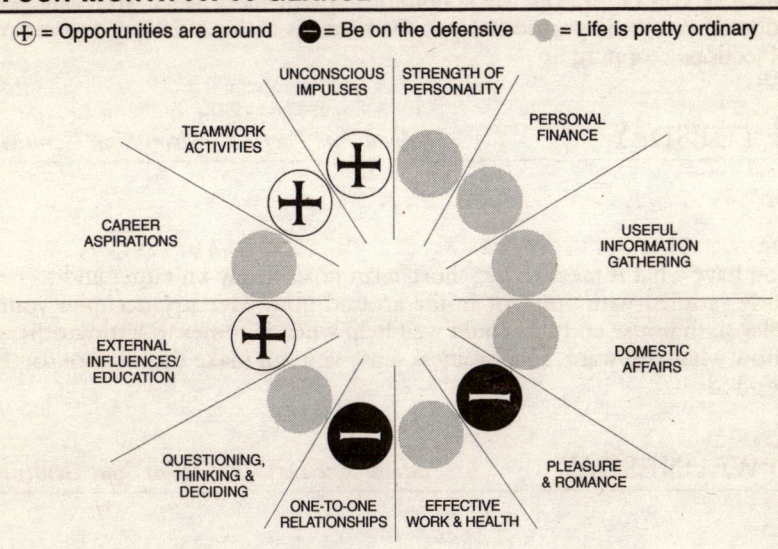

⊕ = Opportunities are around   ⊖ = Be on the defensive   ● = Life is pretty ordinary

- UNCONSCIOUS IMPULSES: ⊕
- STRENGTH OF PERSONALITY: ordinary
- TEAMWORK ACTIVITIES: ⊕
- PERSONAL FINANCE: ordinary
- CAREER ASPIRATIONS: ordinary
- USEFUL INFORMATION GATHERING: ordinary
- EXTERNAL INFLUENCES/EDUCATION: ⊕
- DOMESTIC AFFAIRS: ordinary
- QUESTIONING, THINKING & DECIDING: ordinary
- PLEASURE & ROMANCE: ordinary
- ONE-TO-ONE RELATIONSHIPS: ⊖
- EFFECTIVE WORK & HEALTH: ⊖

SEPTEMBER HIGHS AND LOWS

Here I show you how the rhythms of the Moon will affect you this month. Like the tide, your energies and abilities will rise and fall with its pattern. When it is above the centre line, go for it, when it is below, you should be resting.

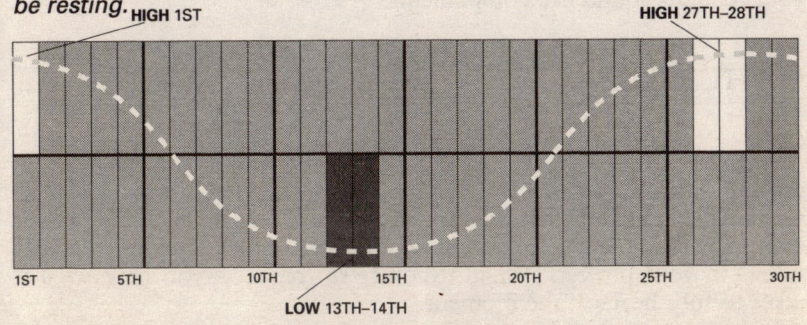

HIGH 1ST

HIGH 27TH–28TH

LOW 13TH–14TH

3 MONDAY *Moon Age Day 21   Moon Sign Taurus*

am ....

pm ....
In terms of your skill to communicate with others it looks as though your personality is especially enhanced today. This is not a time to hold back when it comes to your own opinions, particularly since you can get yourself in a good position to put them across without finding too many objections cropping up.

4 TUESDAY *Moon Age Day 22   Moon Sign Gemini*

am ....

pm ....
You have what it takes to get short-term goals nicely on target and to be fairly satisfied with your lot in life around now. Mercury occupies your solar sixth house and this could well help when it comes to letting others know what you want. In a business sense you can make the most of some good ideas.

5 WEDNESDAY *Moon Age Day 23   Moon Sign Gemini*

am ....

pm ....
You have the ability to be all things to all people under present astrological trends and to make sure the slightly harder and more caustic side of Aries takes a holiday. Because of your charm, this is the time to get what you want, and you should manage to do so in such a way that your requests sound like compliments.

6 THURSDAY *Moon Age Day 24   Moon Sign Cancer*

am ....

pm ....
Certain plans and schemes can now start to take on a practical life of their own. You have scope to exploit new opportunities, and to inculcate others in your projects. When it comes to romance, you have what it takes to turn heads at the moment.

YOUR DAILY GUIDE TO SEPTEMBER 2007

7 FRIDAY
Moon Age Day 25   Moon Sign Cancer

am ....

pm ....
Trends assist you to be very supportive of the ideas of those around you and this is especially true when it comes to family members and friends who have been present for years. Life is a two-way traffic for the sign of Aries right now because you learn as much as you teach – a fact that shouldn't be lost on those you deal with the most.

8 SATURDAY
Moon Age Day 26   Moon Sign Leo

am ....

pm ....
You have a tendency to dominate the limelight at the present time, even if you are not doing anything specific. Your popularity is well marked, and you should be able to get what you want without any real effort at all. Family members may have need of your very specific wise counsel.

9 SUNDAY
Moon Age Day 27   Moon Sign Leo

am ....

pm ....
A boost to your love life is possible this Sunday, particularly if you make sure you have the time necessary to concentrate on this specific area of your life. Set out to have some fun by all means, and make sure that you include your partner. You shouldn't have to say very much because your attitude is very evident.

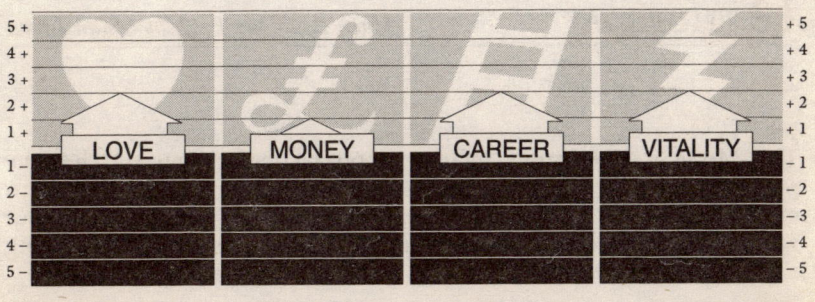

| LOVE | MONEY | CAREER | VITALITY |

10 MONDAY   *Moon Age Day 28   Moon Sign Leo*

am ....

pm ....
You have the ability to portray yourself as being just the right person to be put in charge of some project that requires a patient and practical approach. Advancement is possible for some sons and daughters of Mars, and you can show a very positive approach to almost any situation that comes your way.

11 TUESDAY   *Moon Age Day 29   Moon Sign Virgo*

am ....

pm ....
This period is especially favourable for most sorts of relationships and for establishing a better rapport with ayone who hasn't been your flavour of the month in the past. Whether you like them more or not remains to be seen, but what matters is that you are in a position to form some sort of understanding.

12 WEDNESDAY   *Moon Age Day 0   Moon Sign Virgo*

am ....

pm ....
You could encounter a few obstacles today, and you may feel as if you have little choice but to accept second-best, both from yourself and others. The approaching lunar low is the reason, and your best response is to show a patient attitude and to wait for things to improve. Why not concentrate on pleasing those you love?

13 THURSDAY   *Moon Age Day 1   Moon Sign Libra*

am ....

pm ....
The Moon is now firmly in your opposite zodiac sign and has the potential to bring stumbling blocks that you will have to work hard to get through or round. It might actually be better not to try too hard but rather to wait for better trends before committing yourself to anything that requires real effort.

YOUR DAILY GUIDE TO SEPTEMBER 2007

14 FRIDAY *Moon Age Day 2   Moon Sign Libra*

am ....

pm ....
Trends encourage you to keep to tried and tested paths for just one more day and not to try anything too new or controversial. By taking things steadily you offer yourself the chance to change direction once planetary trends improve. By tomorrow you should be right back on the boil, so avoid getting too frustrated with yourself now.

15 SATURDAY *Moon Age Day 3   Moon Sign Scorpio*

am ....

pm ....
Although one or two of your ideas may be a little impractical at the moment, you do have charm on your side, as well as an ability to exploit the potential you see in others. Don't be too quick to judge a colleague who may be seeing the future somewhat more sensibly than you are.

16 SUNDAY *Moon Age Day 4   Moon Sign Scorpio*

am ....

pm ....
You are in a position to settle things nicely as far as your home life is concerned, even if the more practical side of situations has to wait until tomorrow. If there is still some good weather about, make the most of it and spend time out of doors. For some Aries people this would be a good time for a longer trip or a holiday.

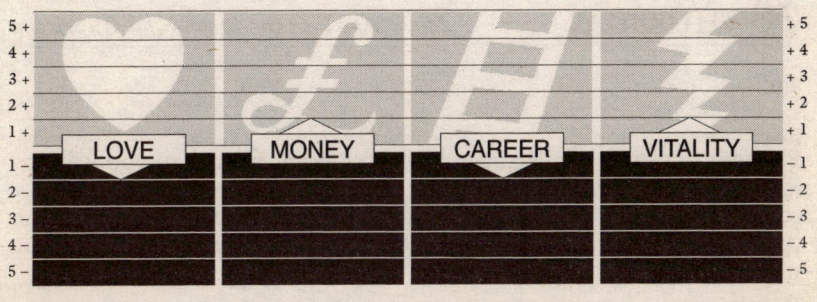

LOVE	MONEY	CAREER	VITALITY

17 MONDAY　　　　*Moon Age Day 5　　Moon Sign Scorpio*

am ....

pm ....
Your ability to act decisively is legendary, and is enhanced no end by the present position of the Sun, which occupies your solar sixth house. This ought to be a good time for romance, and in particular for Aries people who are presently between personal attachments to look around and find a new one.

18 TUESDAY　　　　*Moon Age Day 6　　Moon Sign Sagittarius*

am ....

pm ....
There is information around at this time that you may be able to use to your advantage. By building on platforms you have created earlier you are able to modify your ideas and to react according to circumstances. Aries is shrewd and calculating under present planetary trends, and that spells potential success.

19 WEDNESDAY　　　　*Moon Age Day 7　　Moon Sign Sagittarius*

am ....

pm ....
Mars is now in your solar third house. Although a generally favourable planetary position as far as you are concerned, it may encourage you to be just a little abrupt under certain circumstances. Now is the time to avoid getting into needless arguments, especially with strangers, and to show what a pussycat you are capable of being!

20 THURSDAY　　　　*Moon Age Day 8　　Moon Sign Capricorn*

am ....

pm ....
Relating to others intellectually has never been easier than you will find it to be today. There is an ability to instinctively adopt the right attitude to get on with the prickliest of individuals, and you might even discover that some people are willing to do almost anything just for the chance to make you smile.

YOUR DAILY GUIDE TO SEPTEMBER 2007

21 FRIDAY   *Moon Age Day 9   Moon Sign Capricorn*

am ....

pm ....
You are well geared to achieving significant successes at present. These might be professional in nature, but are just as likely to be associated with sporting activities. You would be wise to be on your guard against those who would try to part you from your money. Any small print needs looking at very carefully indeed.

22 SATURDAY   *Moon Age Day 10   Moon Sign Capricorn*

am ....

pm ....
A time of plain sailing is now possible in terms of personal attachments and you shouldn't have to work very hard to impress anyone. Even if you feel quite impulsive at present, you can make sure that your projects are for the sake of others. What is highlighted most under prevailing astrological trends is your generosity.

23 SUNDAY   *Moon Age Day 11   Moon Sign Aquarius*

am ....

pm ....
By expressing yourself more than adequately, you have what it takes to get your own way and can easily bring others round to your particular point of view. It isn't necessary to bulldoze the world into compliance. All you have to do is to turn on that Aries charm and you can get practically everyone to line up to eat out of your hand.

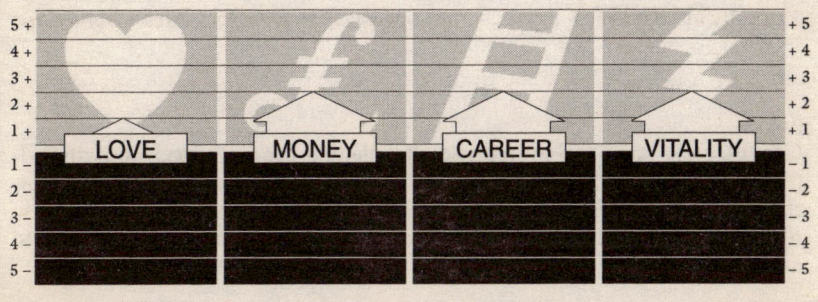

24 MONDAY *Moon Age Day 12   Moon Sign Aquarius*

am ....

pm ....
There are signs that communal and social matters could keep you pretty much on the go, from the moment you get out of bed until you crawl back into it again. Even if this is a busy interlude, you can make it a very happy one too, and a period during which you can lay down fond memories for the future.

25 TUESDAY *Moon Age Day 13   Moon Sign Pisces*

am ....

pm ....
Time spent alone can be quite rewarding. The Moon is in your solar twelfth house and it's only a day or two until the lunar high comes along. In the meantime you have an opportunity to think things through carefully and to sort out the fine details of life – especially ones that are often ignored.

26 WEDNESDAY *Moon Age Day 14   Moon Sign Pisces*

am ....

pm ....
Mood swings are a distinct possibility today, and you might be slightly less approachable than was the case yesterday. With plenty of charm if you choose to use it, there is no real reason for falling out with anyone. It's simply a case of monitoring your actions and correcting them when you know it is necessary.

27 THURSDAY *Moon Age Day 15   Moon Sign Aries*

am ....

pm ....
Get an early start today because the planets are with you and there is plenty you can turn to your advantage. There are situations about now that really do require your personal touch if you are to achieve what you want the most. The lunar high offers you scope for both popularity and know-how.

YOUR DAILY GUIDE TO SEPTEMBER 2007

28 FRIDAY   *Moon Age Day 16   Moon Sign Aries*

am ....

pm ....
If you can keep Lady Luck on your side, you can make sure you are better off than you expected in a financial sense. The attitude of others is really not an issue because you are able to turn most situations around on your own. A day to play for high stakes and show people what Aries is truly capable of achieving.

29 SATURDAY   *Moon Age Day 17   Moon Sign Taurus*

am ....

pm ....
This is a day during which you need to reflect on and understand your own emotions. In particular you would be wise to pay specific attention to the feelings of those around you. Aries is so busy that it sometimes fails to realise that it is treading on the toes of those individuals it relies upon the most. Paying a few compliments would be no bad thing.

30 SUNDAY   *Moon Age Day 18   Moon Sign Taurus*

am ....

pm ....
Certain daily issues come and go, but you can make today enjoyable and make the most of a number of diversions. Don't be too keen to get everything done all at once. Sometimes life offers greater happiness in striving than it does in the sense of achievement that follows a specific project.

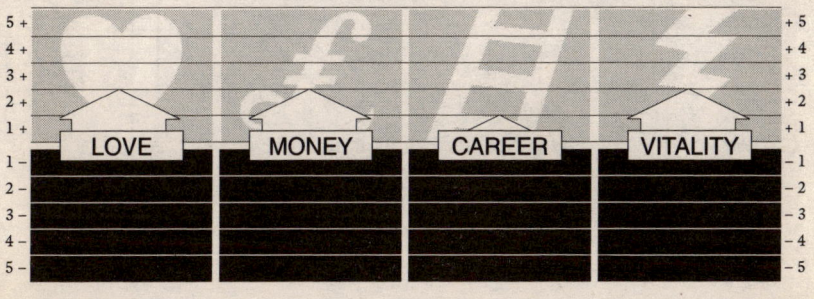

| LOVE | MONEY | CAREER | VITALITY |

October 2007

YOUR MONTH AT A GLANCE

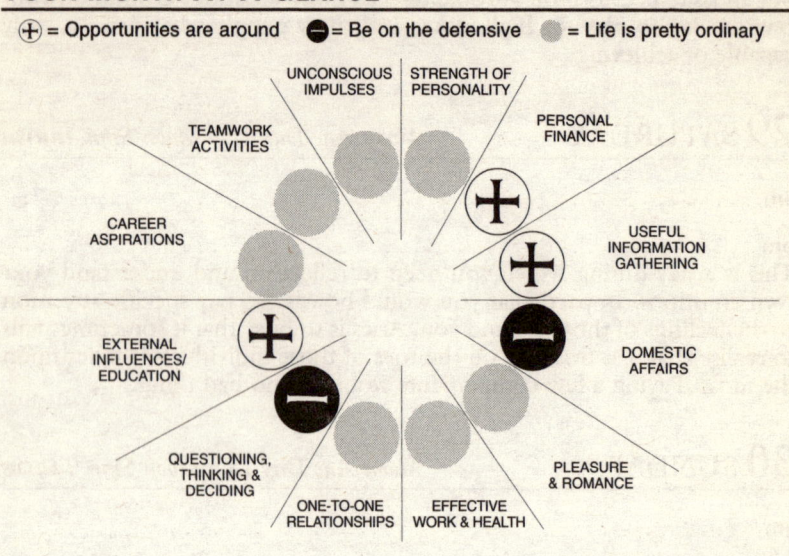

⊕ = Opportunities are around   ⊖ = Be on the defensive   ● = Life is pretty ordinary

- UNCONSCIOUS IMPULSES
- STRENGTH OF PERSONALITY
- TEAMWORK ACTIVITIES
- PERSONAL FINANCE ⊕
- CAREER ASPIRATIONS
- USEFUL INFORMATION GATHERING ⊕
- EXTERNAL INFLUENCES/EDUCATION ⊕
- DOMESTIC AFFAIRS ⊖
- QUESTIONING, THINKING & DECIDING ⊖
- PLEASURE & ROMANCE
- ONE-TO-ONE RELATIONSHIPS
- EFFECTIVE WORK & HEALTH

OCTOBER HIGHS AND LOWS

Here I show you how the rhythms of the Moon will affect you this month. Like the tide, your energies and abilities will rise and fall with its pattern. When it is above the centre line, go for it, when it is below, you should be resting.

HIGH 25TH–26TH

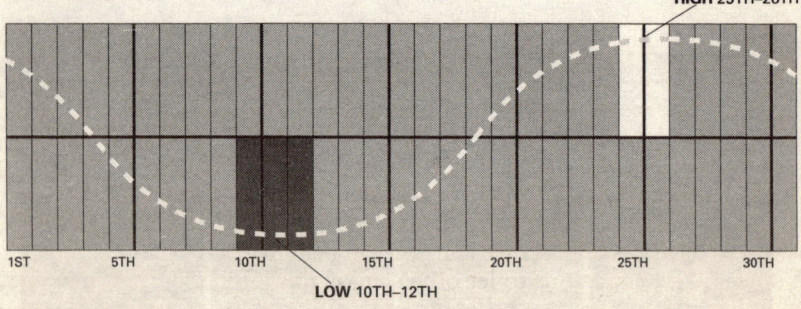

LOW 10TH–12TH

YOUR DAILY GUIDE TO OCTOBER 2007

1 MONDAY   *Moon Age Day 19   Moon Sign Gemini*

am ....

pm ....
It's the first day of a new month and you have a chance to make a really good impression on someone you see as being very significant. Don't go at things like a bull at a gate but show a degree of ingenuity and allow matters to develop slowly. It's a little like catching a fish. Rushing probably doesn't help.

2 TUESDAY   *Moon Age Day 20   Moon Sign Gemini*

am ....

pm ....
You have what it takes to make yourself popular with others today and this really is the key to success for most Aries people around this time. Attitude is very important in professional matters and you can use your natural charm to win through almost any situation. People from the past may well be appearing in your life again now.

3 WEDNESDAY   *Moon Age Day 21   Moon Sign Cancer*

am ....

pm ....
Family relationships could take on a greater importance under present planetary trends, and especially so bearing in mind that the Moon is in your solar fourth house. You can best use these trends by spending some time listening to what your nearest and dearest have to say and leaving more practical matters alone if you can.

4 THURSDAY   *Moon Age Day 22   Moon Sign Cancer*

am ....

pm ....
Trends encourage a happy-go-lucky frame of mind, and you might be thinking seriously about travel. All at once the real practicalities of life seem to have less importance and you can be fully committed to enjoying yourself. You can afford to let others enjoy this interlude with you.

5 FRIDAY
Moon Age Day 23   Moon Sign Leo

am ....

pm ....
Today offers you scope to make those around you as happy as proves to be possible. Your greatest enjoyment could be watching other people enjoy themselves and so everyone wins in the end. In a social sense it is possible for you to begin the weekend one day early and you have what it takes to turn heads romantically.

6 SATURDAY
Moon Age Day 24   Moon Sign Leo

am ....

pm ....
Another lively and enjoyable period is possible, now that the Sun occupies your solar seventh house. The emphasis today is on solid and useful communication. Don't ignore what could turn out to be good advice, even if you think you know better. You might decide to arrange some sort of family outing for tomorrow.

7 SUNDAY
Moon Age Day 25   Moon Sign Leo

am ....

pm ....
Present trends encourage a great need to feel useful, and you may well be pitching around to see to whom you can offer your invaluable services. You think a good deal of yourself at present and there's nothing wrong with that just as long as you come up with the goods when it matters the most.

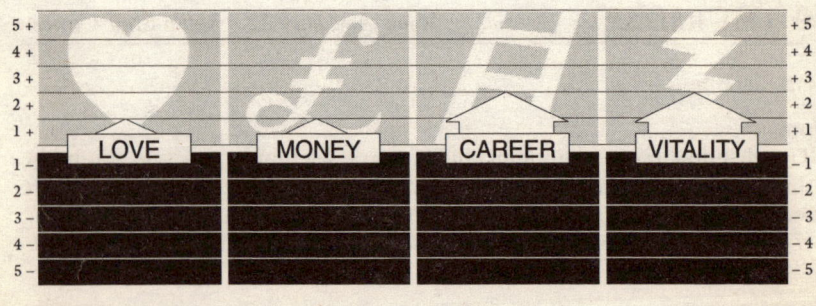

8 MONDAY *Moon Age Day 26   Moon Sign Virgo*

am . . . .

pm . . . .
Emotions might now be running high, especially at home. It could be that certain family members have an idea about how they want to behave, whilst you have a very different notion of what's right. Better to discuss things than to lay down the law. Diplomacy isn't always your middle name, but it should be now.

9 TUESDAY *Moon Age Day 27   Moon Sign Virgo*

am . . . .

pm . . . .
Everything looks as though it will conspire to offer you a potentially positive period as far as work is concerned. Not only is the planet Venus particularly on your side at the moment but the Moon joins in and offers support too. Now you can afford to say what you think and persuade others to give you a really good hearing.

10 WEDNESDAY *Moon Age Day 28   Moon Sign Libra*

am . . . .

pm . . . .
It's true that everyday life might have its drawbacks right now, but you can keep yourself on a roll as far as practical issues are concerned. On those occasions when you know you are out of your depth it might be sensible to enlist a little support, even if that means having to go cap in hand to someone.

11 THURSDAY *Moon Age Day 0   Moon Sign Libra*

am . . . .

pm . . . .
If your influence over life generally is not as good as you might wish, for that you can thank the lunar low, which stays around both today and tomorrow. The best way forward is slowly, and you can achieve a great deal more at the moment by planning than you can by trying to make concrete progress.

12 FRIDAY   ☿   *Moon Age Day 1   Moon Sign Libra*

am ....

pm ....
You are now able to achieve a great deal more in the intimacy stakes, particularly if you are somewhat restricted in other areas of your life. Turning your attention towards love at this time offers a number of benefits. Not least among these is the fact that you can appreciate the warmth that is around you all the time.

13 SATURDAY   ☿   *Moon Age Day 2   Moon Sign Scorpio*

am ....

pm ....
It might be appropriate to make certain changes to your life around this time. For example you may decide this is a good time to begin renovations to your home, or it could be that you want to change your car or even buy some new clothes. Really important issues are best left on the shelf until early next week.

14 SUNDAY   ☿   *Moon Age Day 3   Moon Sign Scorpio*

am ....

pm ....
You might well be able to attract new friends today, especially if you allow yourself to be persuaded to take part in pastimes that you haven't looked at before. There are always new areas of your nature to explore and you seem to have what it takes today to get on well with a whole host of different people.

15 MONDAY ☿ *Moon Age Day 4   Moon Sign Sagittarius*

am ....

pm ....
You benefit from mental stimulation and could do worse that to pit your wits against someone you consider to be a worthy adversary. Aries tendencies are really on display if you are competitive and filled with a desire to be the best. The only disappointment comes when you realise that this is not always the case.

16 TUESDAY ☿ *Moon Age Day 5   Moon Sign Sagittarius*

am ....

pm ....
Rowdy arguments simply will not solve problems at the present time and you would be much better off discussing matters in a sensible way or else withdrawing from situations of confrontation altogether. If you can stay peaceful with yourself and the world at large, you should get a great deal more done.

17 WEDNESDAY ☿ *Moon Age Day 6   Moon Sign Sagittarius*

am ....

pm ....
There are trends about presently that empower you to take actions and to improve certain conditions, especially in your workplace. If routines prove to be something of a bore, it is important to ring the changes as much as possible in order to get the very most out of your life during this interlude.

18 THURSDAY ☿ *Moon Age Day 7   Moon Sign Capricorn*

am ....

pm ....
You may now be sensitive to the moods of others and show a greater tendency than usual to adapt to prevailing circumstances. Even if you can't get everything you want today, if you approach those around you in the proper way you can get very close. Why not look at the present circumstances of a friend and offer some practical help?

19 FRIDAY ☿ *Moon Age Day 8 Moon Sign Capricorn*

am ....

pm ....
Today's insights are steady, enabling you to be a good deal more thoughtful than has been the case across recent days. This is a particularly good time for solving any sort of problem, and it doesn't matter whether this occurs at a practical level or if you are simply spending time with a crossword puzzle.

20 SATURDAY ☿ *Moon Age Day 9 Moon Sign Aquarius*

am ....

pm ....
Trends suggest you have a strong need for friendship, and may well decide to turn to those you have known for some time in order to reassure yourself that they are still as committed to you as they were. As far as this weekend is concerned you may well prefer to have people around you most of the time and should enjoy their presence.

21 SUNDAY ☿ *Moon Age Day 10 Moon Sign Aquarius*

am ....

pm ....
Domestic issues are highlighted, and may take up a great deal of your time today, so you mightn't be able to spend much time thinking about work or purely practical issues. Turn to people you haven't had much to do with of late and learn what they have been doing recently. There could be a revelation in store.

22 MONDAY ☿ *Moon Age Day 11   Moon Sign Pisces*

am . . . .

pm . . . .
A greater desire than usual for solitude is a possibility, and for this you can thank the position of the Moon, which now occupies your solar twelfth house. By being quiet and contemplative you can learn a great deal more about yourself than would be the case if you bluster about aimlessly.

23 TUESDAY ☿ *Moon Age Day 12   Moon Sign Pisces*

am . . . .

pm . . . .
You can move practical matters along quite nicely, even if your nature still doesn't have the edge that it will in a day or two. Acting on impulse is not to be recommended for the moment and you should achieve far more if you let those around you know in advance how you intend to act. There is a strong need for continuity at present.

24 WEDNESDAY ☿ *Moon Age Day 13   Moon Sign Pisces*

am . . . .

pm . . . .
Getting down to the root of personal issues or practical problems is recommended for today. Your intuition is potentially strong and you should not turn away from any deeply held conviction, even on those occasions when you don't understand where the feelings are coming from. Slow and steady wins the race today.

25 THURSDAY ☿ *Moon Age Day 14   Moon Sign Aries*

am . . . .

pm . . . .
The lunar high arrives and offers all manner of new incentives, together with the most positive attitude you have probably experienced during the whole of this month. Now is the time to decide what you want in a practical or professional sense and go for it. Controlling a number of different issues at the same time should be easy.

26 FRIDAY ☿ *Moon Age Day 15   Moon Sign Aries*

am ....

pm ....
If you need assistance you have what it takes to find it at the moment. You can get things to go your way, and can make this one of the best days of October right now. Make the most of the attitude of those with whom you have to deal in a moment-by-moment sense, as it offers you important new incentives.

27 SATURDAY ☿ *Moon Age Day 16   Moon Sign Taurus*

am ....

pm ....
A favourable time is on offer, during which you can strengthen your personal affairs, and today also marks a time when you can look seriously at expenditure and money generally. Although there might be a few dull issues to deal with, in the main you can take this opportunity to ring the changes.

28 SUNDAY ☿ *Moon Age Day 17   Moon Sign Taurus*

am ....

pm ....
There are signs that you might find yourself somewhat at odds with those you have to rely on the most in a momentary sense, and this may be particularly true in your home life. Avoid getting on the wrong side of a particular individual who is in a position to do you some good in the days and weeks ahead. Diplomacy is called for.

29 MONDAY ☿ *Moon Age Day 18   Moon Sign Gemini*

am ....

pm ....
Even if ordinary matters predominate right now, you still have scope to do something more exciting and need to explore a few possibilities. Today offers opportunities to broaden the scope of your interests, and you might also find that romance has a greater part to play in your life than has been the case recently.

30 TUESDAY ☿ *Moon Age Day 19   Moon Sign Gemini*

am ....

pm ....
Advising other people is to the fore today and a few of them will surprise you because they normally seem to give you a wide berth. Don't be too quick to make up your mind about anything. It would be sensible to wait and see in a few specific cases, and even to stop some of your projects altogether.

31 WEDNESDAY ☿ *Moon Age Day 20   Moon Sign Cancer*

am ....

pm ....
Trends suggest that family and personal matters will predominate today, and as the month draws to a close you may also be thinking carefully about those last jobs you want to do around the house before winter begins to settle in. Below the surface there may also be a burning desire to do something quite different and maybe a little exciting.

1 THURSDAY ☿ *Moon Age Day 21   Moon Sign Cancer*

am ....

pm ....
This is a good day for getting together with your partner, family members and close friends. Even if you sense there is plenty to get done in a practical sense, perhaps this really doesn't matter for now. You can afford simply to be yourself and enjoy good company whilst it is on offer. Some real personalities could be entering your life.

2007 HOROSCOPE AND ASTRAL DIARY

2 FRIDAY   ☿   *Moon Age Day 22   Moon Sign Leo*

am ....

pm ....
You can subject certain aspects of your life to a little regeneration at this time and should be quite willing to look at all issues in a very new light. Standard responses probably don't work very well at work, and you need to think of ways to show a greater degree of originality if you can.

3 SATURDAY   *Moon Age Day 23   Moon Sign Leo*

am ....

pm ....
Mercury is now in your solar seventh house, a position from where it stimulates your need for communication and simple companionship. You may be drawn to friends and especially those who have played a part in your life for some years. Be willing to modify your opinions whenever it proves to be advantageous.

4 SUNDAY   *Moon Age Day 24   Moon Sign Virgo*

am ....

pm ....
You can now explore new ways of approaching the world, and have what it takes to come up with revolutionary new ideas that others find difficult to understand. Explaining yourself is what today is all about because you have it within you to bring almost anyone round to your way of thinking if you plan your strategy first.

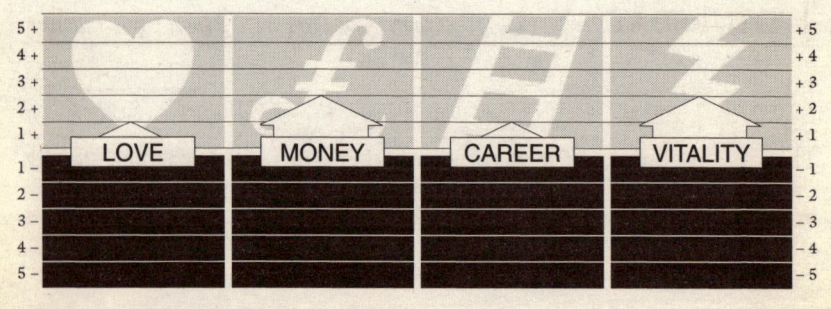

| LOVE | MONEY | CAREER | VITALITY |

November 2007

YOUR MONTH AT A GLANCE

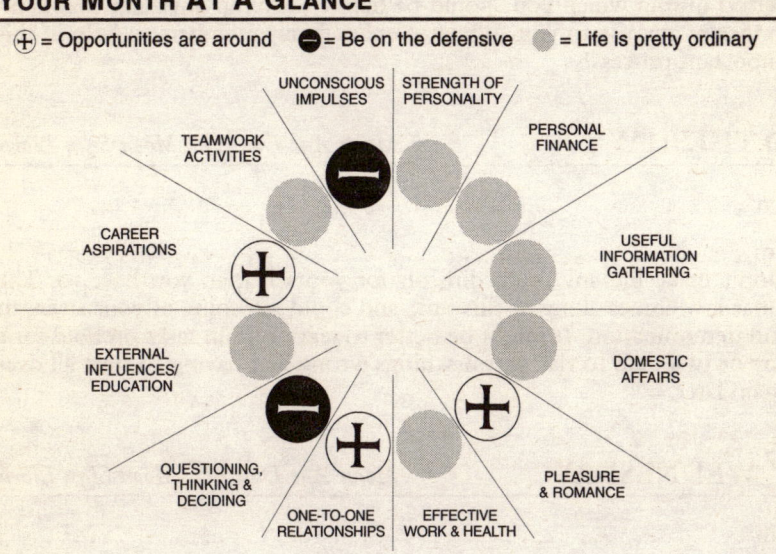

⊕ = Opportunities are around   ⊖ = Be on the defensive   ● = Life is pretty ordinary

- UNCONSCIOUS IMPULSES — ⊖
- STRENGTH OF PERSONALITY
- TEAMWORK ACTIVITIES
- PERSONAL FINANCE
- CAREER ASPIRATIONS — ⊕
- USEFUL INFORMATION GATHERING
- EXTERNAL INFLUENCES/EDUCATION
- DOMESTIC AFFAIRS
- QUESTIONING, THINKING & DECIDING — ⊖
- ONE-TO-ONE RELATIONSHIPS — ⊕
- EFFECTIVE WORK & HEALTH
- PLEASURE & ROMANCE

NOVEMBER HIGHS AND LOWS

Here I show you how the rhythms of the Moon will affect you this month. Like the tide, your energies and abilities will rise and fall with its pattern. When it is above the centre line, go for it, when it is below, you should be resting.

HIGH 21ST–22ND

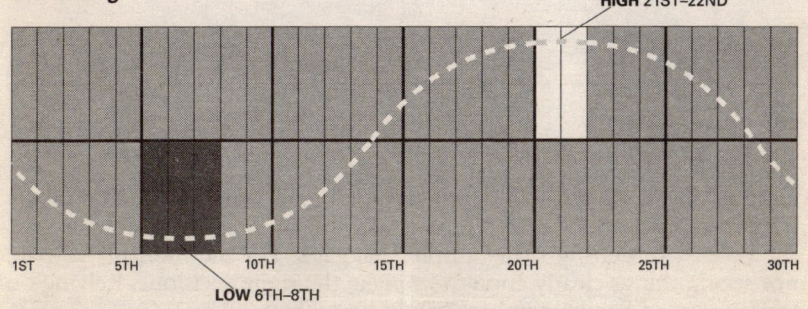

LOW 6TH–8TH

139

5 MONDAY *Moon Age Day 25   Moon Sign Virgo*

am ....

pm ....
You have a chance to get rid of any outworn elements of your life around this time. The present position of the Sun in your solar chart brings a period during which you should be happy to dump anything that is no longer of any use to you. Why not enlist family members to help in this important process?

6 TUESDAY *Moon Age Day 26   Moon Sign Libra*

am ....

pm ....
Don't make life any more difficult for yourself than you have to. The lunar low comes along at this time and could sap some of your strength and determination. It might be better to leave certain tasks on hold for a day or two than to risk getting things wrong and having to start all over again later.

7 WEDNESDAY *Moon Age Day 27   Moon Sign Libra*

am ....

pm ....
A time to stick to tried and tested methods for getting what you want and avoid new fads and fancies. It's the reliable old you that works best at the moment and you should avoid listening to anyone who claims to have discovered every shortcut in the book. You can rely on the friends who have been around you for some time.

8 THURSDAY *Moon Age Day 28   Moon Sign Libra*

am ....

pm ....
Getting ahead should still definitely not be an issue in your mind. By tomorrow things look different and you will once again be able to start the process of getting rid of surplus baggage. For the moment you are not seeing things clearly enough to make the right decisions. Relying on the support of family members would be no bad thing.

9 FRIDAY
Moon Age Day 0   Moon Sign Scorpio

am ....

pm ....
The romantic side of life now comes to the fore, and having left the lunar low behind you, the sky looks blue again, no matter what the weather is doing outside. By being active and enterprising you can show a really positive face to the world and particularly to the person who is most important to you.

10 SATURDAY
Moon Age Day 1   Moon Sign Scorpio

am ....

pm ....
You have scope to influence family members under present trends, and could be spending more time thinking about domestic issues than professional ones. Friends may also be demanding your attention, something that is unlikely to bother you at all whilst Mars occupies your solar fourth house.

11 SUNDAY
Moon Age Day 2   Moon Sign Sagittarius

am ....

pm ....
A real sense of regeneration remains a fundamental component of your life and thinking at this time. This is a phase that is set to continue for at least another week, and marks an important period for coming to terms with the fact that not everything can stay the way it was. A clean sweep is definitely possible.

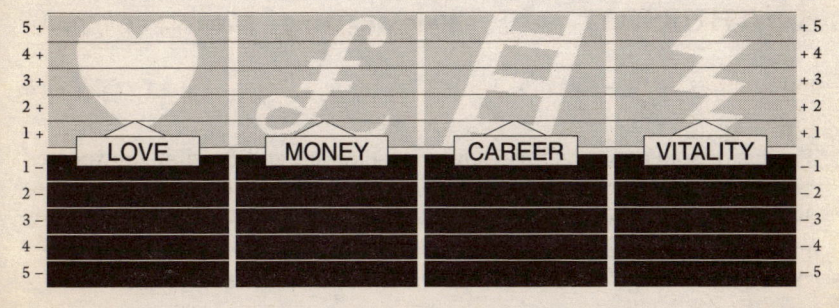

12 MONDAY *Moon Age Day 3   Moon Sign Sagittarius*

am ....

pm ....
Extended travel might seem particularly attractive around now and some Aries subjects will be thinking about journeys that are thousands of miles in length. Beware of being too quick to judge the motivations of colleagues or friends because even if it doesn't look that way, they may actually have your interests at heart.

13 TUESDAY *Moon Age Day 4   Moon Sign Sagittarius*

am ....

pm ....
This has potential to be a wonderful day and one where personal attachments are specifically highlighted. You are able to find exactly the right words to show your nearest and dearest just how important they are to you, and can also show tremendous support to those friends who occupy centre stage in your thinking.

14 WEDNESDAY *Moon Age Day 5   Moon Sign Capricorn*

am ....

pm ....
Trends right now assist you to attune yourself to whatever stimulates others, and so getting on side with them shouldn't be difficult. Your best form of progress now comes through a willingness to share and to be part of something that is definitely bigger than you are. Your charitable qualities are also well accented at present.

15 THURSDAY *Moon Age Day 6   Moon Sign Capricorn*

am ....

pm ....
Professional matters can be given a very pleasant and possibly unexpected boost under present trends. There is now a greater tendency for you to act on impulse and the planetary line-up shows that you can get away with doing so. You can persuade people to respond to your spontaneity and willingly follow your lead.

YOUR DAILY GUIDE TO NOVEMBER 2007

16 FRIDAY   *Moon Age Day 7   Moon Sign Aquarius*

am ....

pm ....
The best gains today can be made by being exactly what you are – an Aries subject. Even if not everyone falls in line with either your thinking or your actions, that doesn't really matter. Those who can are going to be at your shoulder but there may always be one or two people who fall by the wayside.

17 SATURDAY   *Moon Age Day 8   Moon Sign Aquarius*

am ....

pm ....
Venus is now in your solar seventh house, a position from where it has a great bearing on all types of relationships. From the most casual nodding acknowledgement to the love of your life, your ability to get on with those around you is second to none. Much of the progress possible now is related to your present friendliness.

18 SUNDAY   *Moon Age Day 9   Moon Sign Aquarius*

am ....

pm ....
Finances could tend to fluctuate somewhat around now and you need to be just a little more careful in the way you handle money. It could be sensible to ask the advice of someone older or wiser, whilst at the same time giving an eye to the longer-term future and ways you can lay up cash now for decades ahead.

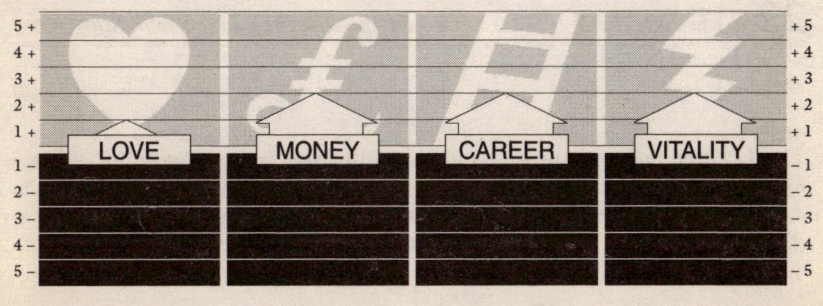

	LOVE	MONEY	CAREER	VITALITY
+5					+5
+4					+4
+3					+3
+2					+2
+1					+1
-1					-1
-2					-2
-3					-3
-4					-4
-5					-5

19 MONDAY *Moon Age Day 10   Moon Sign Pisces*

am ....

pm ....
Social pursuits have potential to capture your imagination and you should be more than willing to join in with whatever is going on in your immediate circle. There are ways in which you can mix business with pleasure, whilst at the same time making profit out of the most unpromising situations. Ingenuity is the key to success at present.

20 TUESDAY *Moon Age Day 11   Moon Sign Pisces*

am ....

pm ....
By tomorrow there is little to stand in your way, but for the first part of today at least you are likely to be showing a much quieter face to the world at large. Thoughtful and even contemplative, you may decide that a particular course of action needs modifying and could spend several hours working things out.

21 WEDNESDAY *Moon Age Day 12   Moon Sign Aries*

am ....

pm ....
The Moon is back in your zodiac sign of Aries and now comes the time for taking those half-exploited ideas and making them work the way you would wish. Almost anything is possible now and something that looked absolutely impossible once upon a time can seem commonplace because of your own effort.

22 THURSDAY *Moon Age Day 13   Moon Sign Aries*

am ....

pm ....
The positive trends continue and extend to the fact that you are able to see ahead positively for the benefit of loved ones as well as for yourself. Acting on impulse is likely to be second nature, and you can show a degree of vivacity that lifts you in the eyes of almost everyone you meet. This is a red-letter day for some Aries people.

YOUR DAILY GUIDE TO NOVEMBER 2007

23 FRIDAY
Moon Age Day 14   Moon Sign Taurus

am ....

pm ....
Getting on side with those around you could be a piece of cake right now. Even people you have always thought of as being awkward in the past can now be brought under your influence, and you have exactly what it takes to make situations work out the way you want them to.

24 SATURDAY
Moon Age Day 15   Moon Sign Taurus

am ....

pm ....
Tensions could arise at home, and these need to be dealt with very carefully if you are to avoid unnecessary and probably slightly destructive rows. Getting your loved ones to see sense may not always be easy, but you have also to be aware that what is self-evident to you might not seem that way to others.

25 SUNDAY
Moon Age Day 16   Moon Sign Gemini

am ....

pm ....
The present position of Venus enhances your naturally romantic frame of mind and assists you to get to grips with personal attachments. The time is right to keep an open mind about necessary changes within your domestic sphere and to look ahead just a little to the festive season, which is only a month away.

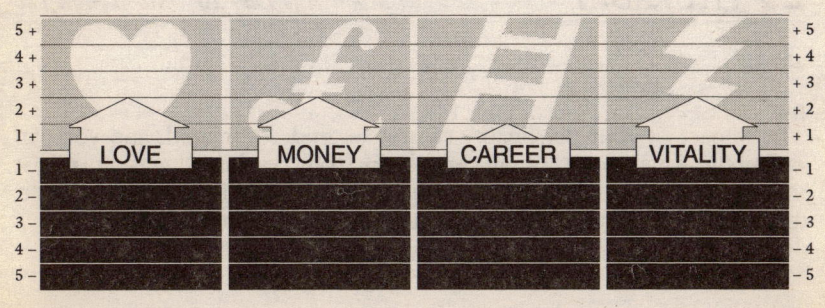

LOVE	MONEY	CAREER	VITALITY

26 MONDAY *Moon Age Day 17   Moon Sign Gemini*

am ....

pm ....
You benefit now from a more open approach and it is vital that you explain yourself to almost everyone. You have what it takes to persuade others to show a great deal of interest in your ideas around this time and to move mountains, if only you employ the more sensible side of your nature. Aries should be well on top under present trends.

27 TUESDAY *Moon Age Day 18   Moon Sign Cancer*

am ....

pm ....
There are some unexpected gains for the taking around now, and some of these will be almost totally unexpected. Showing a great sensitivity to the feelings of others, you can also be active and enterprising for some days to come. Your nature is extremely well balanced at this juncture.

28 WEDNESDAY *Moon Age Day 19   Moon Sign Cancer*

am ....

pm ....
Trends suggest that pressure could be slightly stepped up at home, and it is important not to rise to the bait of people who are being deliberately provocative. Instead of firing from the hip, be willing to look at matters carefully and to reserve your judgement under most circumstances. You can get what you want, but it might take a little while.

29 THURSDAY *Moon Age Day 20   Moon Sign Leo*

am ....

pm ....
The impact of your personality cannot be underestimated, and you can definitely have more of an impression on people than you might immediately realise. Impressing people who really count should be easier, and there is a chance that you can achieve a real advancement soon.

YOUR DAILY GUIDE TO NOVEMBER 2007

30 FRIDAY
Moon Age Day 21   Moon Sign Leo

am ....

pm ....
You can take advantage of a definite peak any time now. There are a number of strong planetary influences working well on your behalf and there are gains to be made in a host of different directions. If there is any problem at the moment it revolves around knowing what to tackle next.

1 SATURDAY
Moon Age Day 22   Moon Sign Virgo

am ....

pm ....
It is possible that at home your emotional needs may conflict with the practical aspects of getting things done. What is necessary today won't be what you want, and a slight conflict could start to develop as a result. Your best approach is to keep ahead of necessary tasks and prepare yourself today for something that is important early next week.

2 SUNDAY
Moon Age Day 23   Moon Sign Virgo

am ....

pm ....
This could be a fairly low-key sort of day, which might seem hard after such a bevy of positive days. All the same there are gains to be made, even if these are only really centred upon your ability to get on the same wavelength as family members and in particular your life partner.

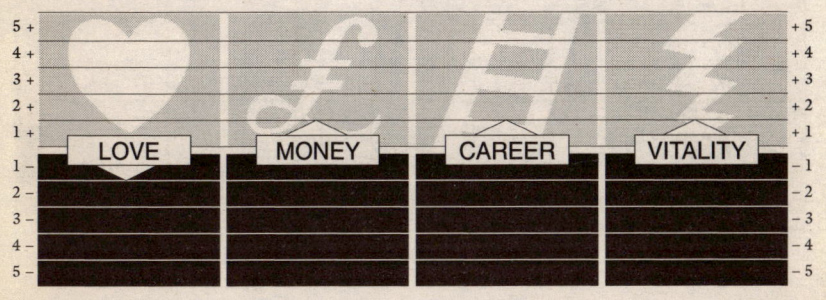

LOVE   MONEY   CAREER   VITALITY

December 2007

Your Month At A Glance

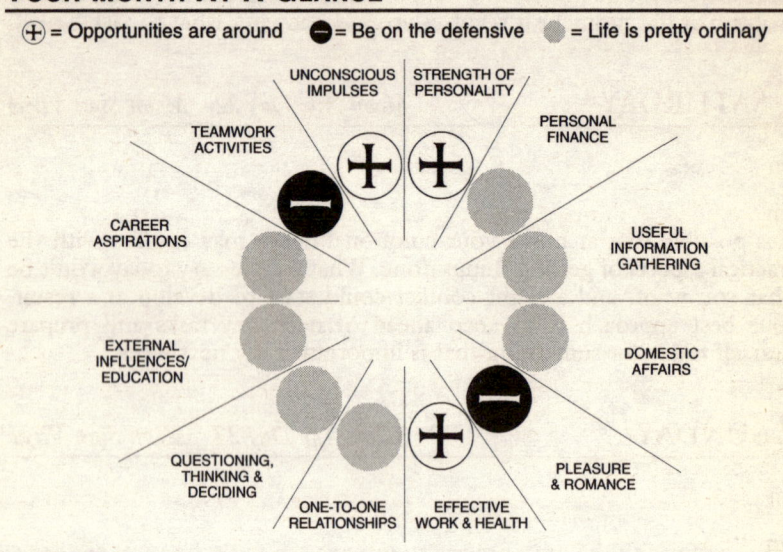

⊕ = Opportunities are around   ⊖ = Be on the defensive   ● = Life is pretty ordinary

- TEAMWORK ACTIVITIES: ⊖
- UNCONSCIOUS IMPULSES: ⊕
- STRENGTH OF PERSONALITY: ⊕
- PERSONAL FINANCE: ordinary
- CAREER ASPIRATIONS: ordinary
- USEFUL INFORMATION GATHERING: ordinary
- EXTERNAL INFLUENCES/EDUCATION: ordinary
- DOMESTIC AFFAIRS: ordinary
- QUESTIONING, THINKING & DECIDING: ordinary
- ONE-TO-ONE RELATIONSHIPS: ordinary
- EFFECTIVE WORK & HEALTH: ⊕
- PLEASURE & ROMANCE: ⊖

December Highs and Lows

Here I show you how the rhythms of the Moon will affect you this month. Like the tide, your energies and abilities will rise and fall with its pattern. When it is above the centre line, go for it, when it is below, you should be resting.

HIGH 18TH–19TH

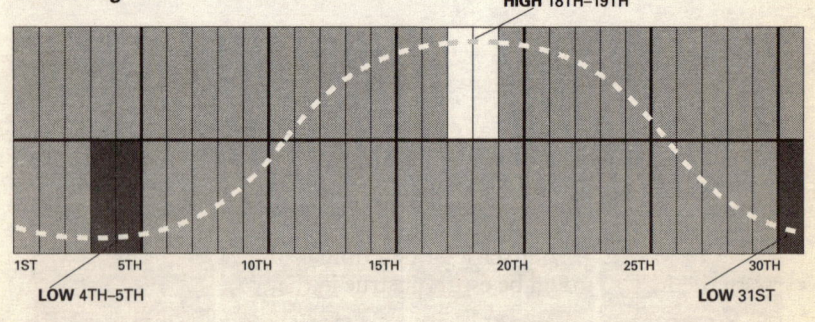

LOW 4TH–5TH

LOW 31ST

3 MONDAY *Moon Age Day 24 Moon Sign Virgo*

am ....

pm ....
Although today might be rather quieter than you expected, it does have its good points. For one thing you can be very attentive to the natures and needs of those around you. Sorting out your own problems today shouldn't really be an issue, but you will be in a position to offer some timely assistance where it's needed the most.

4 TUESDAY *Moon Age Day 25 Moon Sign Libra*

am ....

pm ....
A few compromises might have to be made whilst the lunar low is about and you may also have to work that much harder to get what you want out of today. There are some very useful planetary positions in your solar chart, so it's possible that the position of the Moon will have less of a bearing on you generally than might usually be the case.

5 WEDNESDAY *Moon Age Day 26 Moon Sign Libra*

am ....

pm ....
A day to keep your expectations reasonably low and not to be too anxious to get ahead. You would be better off planning rather than doing anything specific at this time, and allowing those around you to take some of the strain. There ought to be time to think and to recharge batteries that may be flagging a little.

6 THURSDAY *Moon Age Day 27 Moon Sign Scorpio*

am ....

pm ....
Why not get down to basics today and put into action some of the plans you thought about across the last couple of days? You have more energy available now, and a greater sense of determination to get things the way you want them. This would be especially true in the case of your profession.

7 FRIDAY *Moon Age Day 28   Moon Sign Scorpio*

am ....

pm ....
The monetary side of life is well accented at the moment, and it's possible that you have an idea at the back of your head that will see you somehow better off in the days ahead. Ingenuity is second nature to Aries, and especially so under prevailing planetary trends. Now is the time to be bold and determined.

8 SATURDAY *Moon Age Day 29   Moon Sign Scorpio*

am ....

pm ....
This is not a good time to be putting pressure on people at home. You can afford to let things ride for a while and give people the time and space they need to make up their own minds. There are gains to be made from simply watching and waiting, and this applies as much to the practical side of life as to anything else.

9 SUNDAY *Moon Age Day 0   Moon Sign Sagittarius*

am ....

pm ....
Everything that is going on around you can bring its own rewards at this time. Boundless energy is available all of a sudden but you may decide to expend this on family members or friends on a Sunday. Plans for Christmas might be in full swing and there is something warm about the feelings engendered.

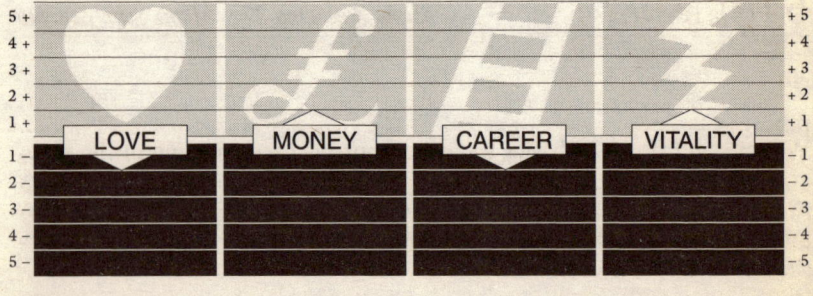

LOVE	MONEY	CAREER	VITALITY

10 MONDAY *Moon Age Day 1   Moon Sign Sagittarius*

am ....

pm ....
You tend to be quite chatty now, and can get a good deal of information simply by being yourself. Although you might decide to defer one or two of your schemes, your mind is probably working overtime and it's fair to suggest that you show a greater ingenuity around this time than has been the case for quite a while.

11 TUESDAY *Moon Age Day 2   Moon Sign Capricorn*

am ....

pm ....
You can be right on the ball when it comes to initiating new schemes, and there isn't much doubt about your capabilities. Bear in mind that others may be watching you closely, and this ought to be one of the best times of the month to get yourself noticed. There are some fairly unexpected gains becoming possible under present planetary trends.

12 WEDNESDAY *Moon Age Day 3   Moon Sign Capricorn*

am ....

pm ....
You could end up allowing powerful emotions to get in the way of your practical common sense, not a state of affairs that is very useful right now. You would be wise to try to stay cool, calm and collected at all times, and if you can't manage to do so, you could spend some time on your own so that others won't see your reactions.

13 THURSDAY *Moon Age Day 4   Moon Sign Capricorn*

am ....

pm ....
The Moon is in your solar eleventh house, a position from where it assists you to bring out the best in yourself. Conforming to the expectations of others may not be easy, but you have sufficient cheek to get away with just about anything now. Your reaction time under all circumstances should be even faster than usual.

14 FRIDAY *Moon Age Day 5 Moon Sign Aquarius*

am ....

pm ....
You can afford to extend yourself into unknown areas and be willing to tackle jobs that you might have shied away from in the past. People you don't see too often could be coming into your life again and are likely to offer you a new way of looking at an old situation. Concentration is good, and your powers of perception highlighted.

15 SATURDAY *Moon Age Day 6 Moon Sign Aquarius*

am ....

pm ....
There are gains to be made if you can avoid the usual tedious routines and try to get as many new influences into your life as proves to be possible. It might be slightly difficult to fall in line with the notions of people you think are idiots, but you can feather your own nest by showing a willingness to follow their lead.

16 SUNDAY *Moon Age Day 7 Moon Sign Pisces*

am ....

pm ....
This is a potentially favourable time for financial matters and especially for looking again at any issues from the past that have been shelved for some time. Ingenuity is a hallmark of your nature at the moment and you have what it takes to put in that extra bit of thought that can make all the difference in the end.

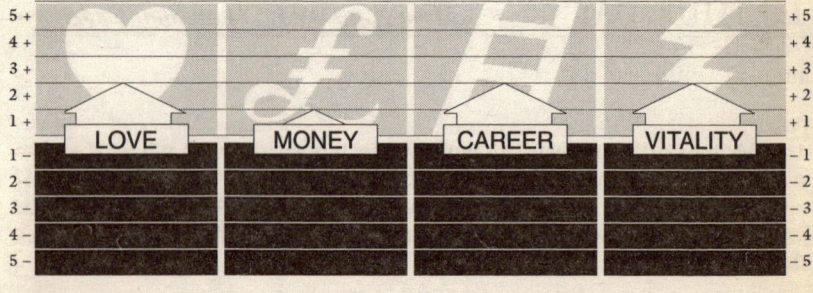

LOVE	MONEY	CAREER	VITALITY

17 MONDAY
Moon Age Day 8   Moon Sign Pisces

am ....

pm ....
The Moon is now in your solar twelfth house and this makes for an excellent day to be working on your own. It isn't that you have any difficulty getting on with others. On the contrary, your popularity could be going off the scale at the moment. It's simply that you may be more efficient when tackling things in your own way.

18 TUESDAY
Moon Age Day 9   Moon Sign Aries

am ....

pm ....
The lunar high assists you to tackle several different tasks at the same time. You have what it takes to get ahead in almost any sphere of your life and demonstrate just how capable you are when it matters the most. If thoughts of Christmas are on your mind, why not sort out a few practical necessities today?

19 WEDNESDAY
Moon Age Day 10   Moon Sign Aries

am ....

pm ....
You should still be in good form and able to tackle things that would have intimidated even you earlier in the month. With everything to play for and plenty of energy at your command, this is the time to put in that essential push ahead of the festive season. There should also be hours available in which to simply enjoy yourself.

20 THURSDAY
Moon Age Day 11   Moon Sign Taurus

am ....

pm ....
Your practical energies are best directed towards work, and you should still be feeling on top form. Even if you have difficulty getting on side with one or two people, when it matters the most you can adapt your own nature to suit theirs. Trends encourage you to be especially compassionate at the moment.

21 FRIDAY
Moon Age Day 12   Moon Sign Taurus

am ....

pm ....
You need to think fairly seriously about your own career direction at present, though this may not be easy at a time of year when there are many distractions pressing in on you. Prepare yourself for an enforced lay-off during the Christmas period, and make sure that you have your plans well laid in advance.

22 SATURDAY
Moon Age Day 13   Moon Sign Gemini

am ....

pm ....
Relationships are highlighted, and this area of life is coming good at just the right time. You should be present to help with arrangements and can even be experiencing distinct periods of nostalgia – something that doesn't happen very much to Aries people. Pleasing others seems to be very significant at present.

23 SUNDAY
Moon Age Day 14   Moon Sign Gemini

am ....

pm ....
Trends suggest you will enjoy being on the move and won't be at all pleased if you find yourself being restricted in any way. Don't be too worried if something you see as important has to take second place to pleasing family members. There is always another day, and you don't want to appear too distracted to join in socially.

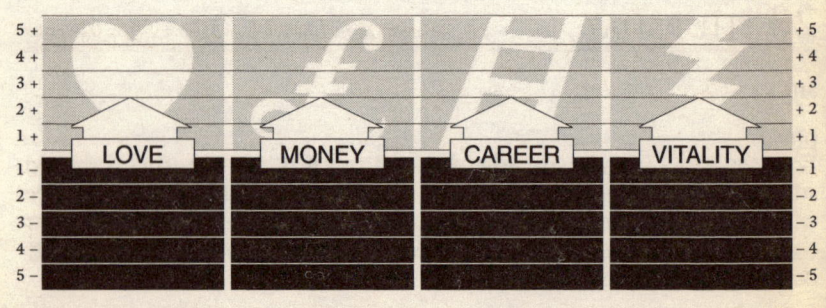

LOVE	MONEY	CAREER	VITALITY

24 MONDAY *Moon Age Day 15   Moon Sign Cancer*

am ....

pm ....
The Moon is now in your solar fourth house and that puts you firmly in the area of home and family as far as your thinking is concerned. This might encourage you to be quieter and more contemplative than has been the case in the recent past and to show the greatest consideration possible to the needs of others.

25 TUESDAY *Moon Age Day 16   Moon Sign Cancer*

am ....

pm ....
Although Christmas Day could prove to be extremely happy, it also has its demands. Your own ruling planet Mars is conjunct with the Moon in your solar fourth house and so a good deal of patience will be necessary. Add to this a few minor frustrations and it's clear that you have your work cut out in order to smile all day.

26 WEDNESDAY *Moon Age Day 17   Moon Sign Leo*

am ....

pm ....
A marvellous sense of emotional closeness becomes possible, and with less pressure on you, this might be the most enjoyable of the two main holidays of Christmas. You could feel drawn towards intimate moments and show a warmth and sensitivity for which your zodiac sign of Aries is not generally famous.

27 THURSDAY *Moon Age Day 18   Moon Sign Leo*

am ....

pm ....
A lively and extroverted influence is brought about by the changing position of the Moon. Active and enterprising, you need to be out of the house and finding ways to use up some of the surplus energy that surges through you at the moment. Even if you still show significant sensitivity, it could be overpowered by a need to act.

28 FRIDAY   *Moon Age Day 19   Moon Sign Leo*

am ....

pm ....
You can make this quite a progressive time in a general sense, which is only slightly spoiled if there are demands being made of you that are difficult to deal with. There is something of a split between your sense of loyalty to your family and your simple, raw need to get on with life at a practical level.

29 SATURDAY   *Moon Age Day 20   Moon Sign Virgo*

am ....

pm ....
The domestic sphere might be upset by arguments that are not only needless but actually totally ridiculous. The best way forward for you is to refuse to be drawn into such situations. Playing the honest broker is fine, but not if this means you have to take sides in such a way that you become directly involved.

30 SUNDAY   *Moon Age Day 21   Moon Sign Virgo*

am ....

pm ....
It is obvious that you have what it takes to keep up a very high profile today and to attract plenty of attention. With the festivities probably still going on all around you, it seems as though you are tired of enjoying yourself and want to get on with some of the practical plans that have been on your mind for a while.

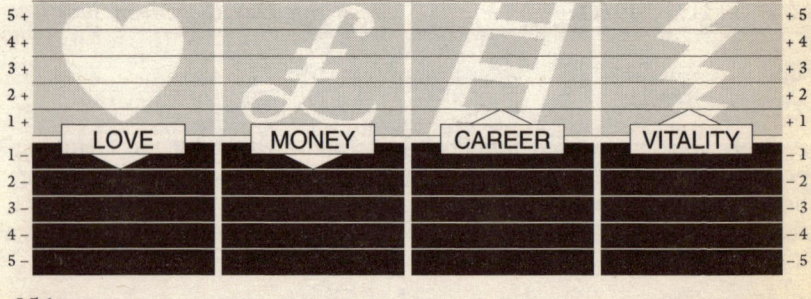

31 MONDAY *Moon Age Day 22   Moon Sign Libra*

am ....

pm ....

It might not be easy to be happy-go-lucky at a time when the Moon occupies your opposite zodiac sign. All the same you should be able to put a smile on your face and to enjoy the passing of the old year. Don't be surprised if you prefer the company of people you know very well because you may shun strangers slightly.

RISING SIGNS FOR ARIES

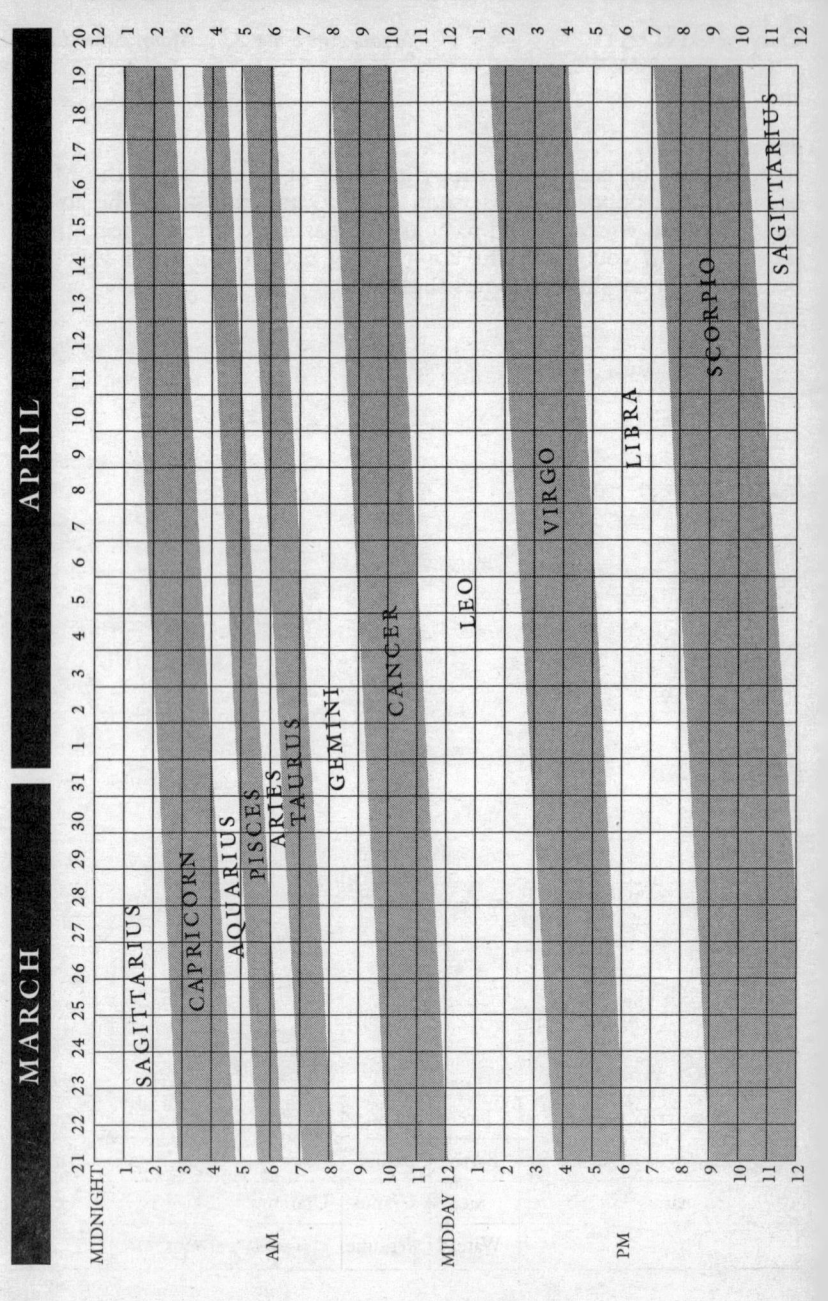

THE ZODIAC, PLANETS AND CORRESPONDENCES

The Earth revolves around the Sun once every calendar year, so when viewed from Earth the Sun appears in a different part of the sky as the year progresses. In astrology, these parts of the sky are divided into the signs of the zodiac and this means that the signs are organised in a circle. The circle begins with Aries and ends with Pisces.

Taking the zodiac sign as a starting point, astrologers then work with all the positions of planets, stars and many other factors to calculate horoscopes and birth charts and tell us what the stars have in store for us.

The table below shows the planets and Elements for each of the signs of the zodiac. Each sign belongs to one of the four Elements: Fire, Air, Earth or Water. Fire signs are creative and enthusiastic; Air signs are mentally active and thoughtful; Earth signs are constructive and practical; Water signs are emotional and have strong feelings.

It also shows the metals and gemstones associated with, or corresponding with, each sign. The correspondence is made when a metal or stone possesses properties that are held in common with a particular sign of the zodiac.

Finally, the table shows the opposite of each star sign – this is the opposite sign in the astrological circle.

Placed	Sign	Symbol	Element	Planet	Metal	Stone	Opposite
1	Aries	Ram	Fire	Mars	Iron	Bloodstone	Libra
2	Taurus	Bull	Earth	Venus	Copper	Sapphire	Scorpio
3	Gemini	Twins	Air	Mercury	Mercury	Tiger's Eye	Sagittarius
4	Cancer	Crab	Water	Moon	Silver	Pearl	Capricorn
5	Leo	Lion	Fire	Sun	Gold	Ruby	Aquarius
6	Virgo	Maiden	Earth	Mercury	Mercury	Sardonyx	Pisces
7	Libra	Scales	Air	Venus	Copper	Sapphire	Aries
8	Scorpio	Scorpion	Water	Pluto	Plutonium	Jasper	Taurus
9	Sagittarius	Archer	Fire	Jupiter	Tin	Topaz	Gemini
10	Capricorn	Goat	Earth	Saturn	Lead	Black Onyx	Cancer
11	Aquarius	Waterbearer	Air	Uranus	Uranium	Amethyst	Leo
12	Pisces	Fishes	Water	Neptune	Tin	Moonstone	Virgo

Foulsham books can be found in all good bookshops or direct from **www.foulsham.com**